THE RELUCTANT ARISTOCRAT

THE RELUCTANT ARISTOCRAT

Mary, Marchioness of Huntly, 1822-1893

DR MAXINE EZIEFULA

Maxine Eziefula

Maria Antoinetta Gordon
*Huntingdonshire Archives and Local Studies, Huntly family album
(1860-1870). Front cover image: Maria Antoinetta Gordon
Huntingdonshire Archives and Local Studies, Huntly family album
(1860-1870)*

Copyright © 2022 by Maxine Eziefula

All rights reserved. No part of this book may be reproduced in any manner whatsoever without written permission except in the case of brief quotations embodied in critical articles and reviews.

First Printing, 2022

Contents

1	Who Was Mary?	16
2	The Books: Why? What? When? Where? How?	54
3	The Books: Consolidating Faith	99
4	The Books: Questioning Faith	146
5	The Gardens	186
6	Woman Amongst Women	227
7	Suffocation	265

Preface

There are many who think that no one ever wrote a line, even in the most private diary, without the belief, or the hope, that it would be read.
(Martineau; Chapman, Harriet Martineau's Autobiography, 1877) vol 1, p.274. (11/15.5.1877)

Gathered lichen & small ivy leaves with the idea of making the device of a cross covered with lichen & supporting ivy - with the words 'simply to the cross I cling'.
Mary's Diaries (3/22.5.1856)

We will never know for sure whether Mary expected her diary to be read by others, but the fact that she did not destroy it, but entrusted it to her eldest daughter, instructing her to make the decision concerning its fate, suggests the answer. The second quote from the diary provides a clear certainty - that at the centre of her being, beyond words and nature, was her Christian faith, even more precious than either.

I wrote a thesis which discussed elite women enjoying and cultivating their gardens in the nineteenth century and, when, during my search for material, I found the diaries of Maria Antoinetta Huntly (known since childhood as Mary) I was quickly captivated by her passionate love of plants and gardening and her clear and thoughtful accounts of daily life. Eleven volumes represented her childhood from November 19th 1832 until her marriage in 1844, and sixteen volumes covered the subsequent period until 4th July 1893, some weeks before her death. All revealed a great love of the natural world. I scoured the diaries from beginning to end, skimming some sections, especially those describing purely social occasions, and focusing more closely on others. I saw how one woman felt about her gardens and about plants, wild and cultivated, and how she collected, grew and documented them. In my thesis, Mary was referred to by her full name, Maria, to distinguish her from another character with a similar name. Although the thesis was focused on gardening and botanising, inevitably I became aware of various other aspects of Mary's life. These included her families, both of childhood and marriage, her social activities, many of which were dutifully and reluctantly performed, her extensive reading and her religious musings and practices. All these feature in this book, but it is her Christian belief which is now the main focus.

I have been unable to suppress my fascination with Mary's self-deprecating accounts and quiet, unshakeable devotion to her faith, and my admiration at the capabilities of her mind. At first, I thought her beguiling in personality, the writer of an informative and very readable diary, but conventional in many ways, over-dutiful, often anxious to please and fussy over religion-similar, in fact, to many women of her time, though perhaps more so to those of the middle class. Whilst the diary was a rich source of her gardening and botanising practices, Mary herself, I felt, was of limited interest and, furthermore, for much of the latter part of her lifetime, her fortunes were waning at various levels, her days often weary, her spirit disillusioned. Sometimes, however, that which seems dim and understated when first perceived begins to shine brighter when under more prolonged survey. Mary and her life have seeped into my consciousness over a period of years- a photo of her adorns my lounge; I think of her often; I wonder at her excellence in writing, her extensive reading, her intellectual breadth and depth, so modestly understated, her quiet persistence in Christian practice amidst the flurry of worldly pleasures that surrounded her.

To some all this may not seem enticing, but I can simply state the case as it is and present Mary, not only as a passionate gardener and botanist and the provider of an unsurpassed account of a lifetime's reading, but also a 'person of interest' in her own right and, through her diary, a gentle companion to the reader, frank and very vulnerable. After 'living' with Mary for some years, my obsession with her has not wavered, but my view of her has changed a little. I am more critical of her passivity in worldly matters, which sometimes seems to cast her too much as a victim, of her lack of understanding of the preoccupations of others less unworldly than herself, and of some of her intolerances, which are explored in the next chapter. Her religious punctiliousness, however, has irritated me less. Her faith was lifelong, habitual and undramatic, but I perceive her as one of the brighter lights in Christ's kingdom. Unsure of herself as she always seemed to be, she was, nonetheless, an oasis of sanity and depth in a shallow, confused and sceptical world.

For most of her life, Mary did not seek publicity; nor did she do much that was of interest to a broad public, whether through lack of inclination or failure of confidence. Thus little has been written of her and little interest shown in her life. However, she appears in the biography of her half-sister Charlotte (1812-1895), by Revel Guest and Angela John, and in the autobiographies of her eldest son, Charles, most often referred to in later years as Huntly. She is also mentioned in her younger sister Elizabeth's diary, those of her children, Mary, Grace and Ethel; and also those of Charlotte and her husband, the 10th Marquis of Huntly (1792-1863).

Her botanical researches are documented in an article by Sheail and Wells, *The Marchioness of Huntly: The Written Record and the Herbarium*; she had produced an impressive herbarium of British and Central European plants. An article by her gardener, Harding, also appeared in 1892 in the *Journal of the Royal Horticultural Society*, with the announcement of a prize for *Conifers, Collection of Fresh Cones and Branches with Foliage* awarded the previous year. Thus it was the Royal Horticultural Society that finally honoured Mary. She was awarded the Veitch Memorial Medal for the conifers, submitted for exhibition, and a prize of £5. At this later period in Mary's life, this acknowledgment of her achievement was important to her and she described herself in her diary as **rather put out by the non-recognition of the planting & ownership of the conifers here in the newspaper reports which give Harding alone all the glory** (15/9.10.1891), this providing a good example of the longstanding perception that head gardeners were taking undue credit for exhibits, indeed, that the gardens were 'owned' by their gardeners unless the actual owners asserted themselves.

Mary also wrote and illustrated a small book, entitled *Thoughts in Verse Upon Flowers of the Field* (1866), which was printed by Day & Son, and given limited circulation on a basis of personal contacts, a practice not uncommon at this period, and possibly appealing to Mary's private nature as being merely semi-public. She wrote initially, **Showed my illuminated pages to Day & Son who encouraged publishing.** (6/1.4.1864). Later, she mentioned *a note from Mrs. Coke to say that the Princess wishes for 2 copies of the Book & is pleased with the illustrations.* (7/16.5.1865). She reported that **Mrs. C. also takes a copy** and that she *sent the book & prospectus to Mrs. Sarah Spencer* (7/16.5.1865). However, it seemed to be all downhill after that. She told how *I left my book with a note from which I gathered that it had not been very popular at Cambridge - but poor dear Lady E. offers to exert herself to get names in London!* (7/23.5.1865). More than two years later she had a *personal interview with H- Day & Son.* (8/29.10.1867). The following year, through half-sister Charlotte, Mary contacted a Mr. Dallas asking for advice about disposing of copies. (8/27.11.1868). The slow process continued; more than a couple of years further on, she *wrote to Victoria [Greke] sending her 6 copies of Flowers of the Field.* (9/2.4.1871)

She also reported *writing the opening of a novel,* but there seems to have been no progress made. (10/18.1.1875). Other attempts at publication were no more successful. Shortly before her death, Mary wrote a book of comical historical verses for children. She wrote out *The Invasion of Britain by the Romans*, the first portion of *A Comic History of England* in verse **having put the lines together during my night vigils**, (16/6.12.1892), and mentioned **George who read through my lines without being much bored**. (16/20.12.1892). She clearly was not hopeful and later sought **the opinion of my sister Charlotte & her husband as to whether they were worthy of being printed or published**. (16/21.4.1893). Later, she reported: **Heard from Blanche Ponsonby enclosing a letter from Mr. John Murray saying he has read through the rhymes in English History & does not advise their publication which quite accords with my own opinion & is a relief to me.** (16/8.5.1893). The letter from the publisher, John Murray had stated with clear gallantry:

> "I would dissuade any friend from publishing these verses on English History. The teaching of History is now conducted (or at least claims to be conducted) on such scientific lines, and there is so fierce a competition among 'primers' and 'manuals' ... that any newcomer is sure to be subjected to very rigorous & unfriendly criticism." (16/ 8.5.1893)

Mr. Collins of Peterborough wrote soon to Mary in similar tone, "*I return your verse with a few short criticisms.*" (16/15.6.1893). He followed this up some days later with the following remark:

> "I think perhaps the second of your two titles would be best- when you call the volume simply 'Rhyme (or verses) in English History'... with regard to publishing I honestly don't think ..." (16/ 2.7.1893)

There are, thus, various public records of Mary aside from her listings in records of aristocracy, but nothing close to the accolades afforded to Charlotte, known in her first marriage as Lady Charlotte Guest and, in her second, as Lady Charlotte Schreiber, whose biography is written and who was famed for her pioneering work in various fields, at a time when there were considerable barriers to public achievement for women. In the context of her class, her time, her family, her gender, Charlotte overstepped a number of boundaries. The relationship, and sometimes the misunderstandings and disagreements between the two half-sisters, are enlightening as to the fundamental differences between them in both situation and personality, and this is explored in later chapters.

The seed of this book was planted quite a number of years ago by a supervisor of my thesis, Professor Kate Retford, who once suggested that an interesting study could be made of the reading matter meticulously recorded in Mary's diary. Although this was not my preoccupation at that time, the seed slowly grew and I looked afresh at the diaries with this new focus, and gradually compiled a very substantial bibliography according to Mary's accounts of what she read. This book explores the world, social, religious, intellectual and physical, into which Mary was born, her inherited positioning within that world and how she moved, acted and felt within it; also her gardening, her study of natural history, her life in family and estate, and her reading. Through and above all is her relationship with her Saviour.

As well as documenting what Mary read in her lifetime, I

have sought to understand the role and context of her reading - why, what when, where and how she read, and how she reacted when, indeed, she did record a reaction. I have noted how her appetite for books, including many that were challenging to her faith and way of life, remained undiminished through life and increased after her husband's death. I have also looked at the relationship between her reading and her other major preoccupations, especially gardening/botany and religion. The triad of Christianity, gardening and natural history, and reading links her with many in her times, especially a certain group known as 'botanical clergyman,' several of whom Mary knew or became acquainted with.

It is worth quoting at length, historian of reading, Amy Cruse who, whilst acknowledging the serious reading undertaken by a significant number of Victorian women, wrote, referring to readers of both sexes, *"It is unfortunate for our purposes that so few Victorian readers have put their reactions to the books they read on record."*

She continues later:

"The diary habit is not a common one, and even industrious diarists often make little mention of books. Only a few, like Lady Frederick Cavendish and Miss Mary Gladstone, give full and interesting details concerning their reading. Biographies, for our purpose, are equally disappointing. Even if they give, as they often do, the weighty works which their subject studied as part of his education, they make only casual mention of a few of the books he read for his pleasure and entertainment."

This is not true of all Victorian diarists, especially male ones, and some - Henry Fynes Clinton (1781-1852), Lord Macaulay (1800-1859), Sir Gerald Graham (1831-1899) and Thomas Green (1769-1825) are mentioned by Arthur Ponsonby in his review of English diaries, for their prolific and sometimes extended discussion of books. Also, as more hidden diaries emerge and as the study of the history and nature of reading continues to expand, this picture may change. However, Mary, Marchioness of Huntly's diary is outstanding in the regularity and comprehensiveness of its account, extending for a lifetime, and supreme in showing what one well-educated women of the nineteenth century read in her life.

The diaries of Lady Frederick Cavendish and Mary Gladstone, whilst providing carefully thought out, sometimes lengthy personal responses to books, which are invariably interesting to read, do not, nonetheless, provide this consistency and could not supply material for a comprehensive bibliography. How typical Mary was in her reading is hard to gage. Undoubtedly, true to their reputation, many women, especially those of the middle classes, would have confined themselves largely to fiction- mainly novels, often supplied by circulating libraries, such as Mudie's, but it seems likely that there was a minority, especially in the better educated upper classes who, like Mary, and like Cavendish and Gladstone, explored much more widely.

Mary's diary tells a human story with the common ingredients- pathos, irony, some tragedy, some drama and many fairly 'uneventful' hours and days which, in most cases, are faithfully and mechanically recorded in her diary; at the centre is a woman's battle with overwhelming adversity, a battle against loss and weariness, illness and disillusion, in which she was upheld by her Christian faith. Mary was no heroine in the conventional sense, for she often failed in her worldly objectives, had marked weaknesses and, in contrast to Charlotte, has fallen into an obscure place in history. Were it not for her class status, with the leisure and disposition to write a diary, we are unlikely to be much aware of her; but our account of this woman, will demonstrate how all this does not make her less interesting- indeed, in many respects, much more so.

Privileged as she was, Mary had limited appreciation of the elevation of her class position, though weighed down by its duties. Many could have envied her lifestyle and assets, the large mansion, servants and invitation to balls, though these were not generally what she valued. Still we can identify with her emotions and her struggles; her often perplexed and frankly fumbling approach to life, especially in adulthood, reflects, if not the persona of most of us, at least the vulnerable underside. We can find comfort and fellowship in Mary as a model of endurance- not a glamorous role, but one which can nourish the spirit.

This book does not relish celebrity; there are enough works that do so. Despite her class and privileges, Mary was 'ordinary', but extraordinary in her honest self-portrayal in her diary as a naked soul (unfashionable though this language may now be in relation to postmodernist analysis of the subject). She was unmaterialistic, humble and self-critical, bearing witness, not only to her dutiful Christian nature, but also her naturally simple attitudes to everyday matters - all this, in spite of the deep and active intellect displayed in her reading and comments. Mary, by virtue both of her social position and the times and circumstances in which she lived, was subject in later life to considerable upheavals, including a dramatic decline in fortunes, the deaths of husband and children, and profound challenges to her self-esteem; but she shied away from drama, yearning for life to continue quietly and at an even pace.

Interest does not lie only in the spectacular. Sometimes the more 'ordinary' subject can come closer to the heart and the understanding. Missed goals and disappointed hopes are familiar to most of us and the writer who can present her/himself frankly and without self-embellishment can appeal to our common humanity, however different our background may be. The distance in time, the trappings of aristocracy are no obstacles in the case of a woman who never seemed fully to believe in herself and, whilst enjoying many of her privileges, especially her beautiful large gardens and her interesting circle of relatives, friends and associates, held the futile and empty social round somewhat in contempt.

The ordinary and the everyday as opposed to the heroic was gradually becoming a focus of religion, especially within evangelicalism. This subject is raised in Chapter 3, but it is sufficient to point out here how the story of Mary illustrates this ethic. Far from ordinary in status and heritage and accustomed to a high standard of living, she discarded and disowned much of this inflated image, partly from inclination, partly from religious belief and partly from necessity, as her fortunes declined. Her repeated attempts to save her family estates in the many difficult years following her husband's death, were ultimately doomed to failure. Mary's life, however, has its positive revelations - her botanical achievements, the discovery of the quantity and depth of her reading, which is recorded in the diary; the unfailing steadfastness of her Christian faith.

After noting what Mary read, I have read as much as possible of this myself, preference being given, in most cases, to versions published close to the date on which Mary is recorded to have read them, even if it was not always possible to know or read the versions she read. I have focused on books of all kinds, including poetry. More often than not I have accessed the material online and am indebted especially to Internet Archive; also to Project Gutenberg and Google Books. Of the enormous number of texts, some I have read carefully, others skimmed, some not read at all, but I believe I have shared Mary's reading experience quite fully. My mirroring of Mary's reading has been supplemented by some of my own. This has included books and articles about the period and its intellectual/scientific, and especially its religious preoccupations; other output of the authors that Mary read; books about Mary's family; and general theoretical works on autobiography and works cited.

Some other female diarists, also talented in gardening or natural history, appeared in my original thesis and there is occasional reference to them here. These are Charlotte, Mary's half-sister (already introduced), Anne Lister (1791-1840), who became owner of Shibden Hall, West Yorkshire and Emily Shore (1819-1839), resident for most of her short life at Woodbury Hall in Bedfordshire. Charlotte is referred to more often, because of some shared family experiences, but also in terms of a contrasting frame of mind and life trajectory.

Quotations from Mary's diary are in both **bold and italics** and are dated within the text. In the case of the adult diaries, volume numbers are given before the dates, though the pre-marriage volumes are unnumbered. Only the first quote from Mary's diary in each chapter is referenced as a quote from her diary. Quotes not attributed to other diarists may be assumed to be from Mary's diary.

Quotations from Mary's reading material are distinguished in this book by italic print. The date of first reading or first mention by Mary is given; although books were often read over a period and a number of books read in childhood were read again later with her children, dates of continued or later reading even when in a different form of publication are not given, unless there are substantial differences in content. Quotations from books within the text are generally ordered by the date in which they were read by Mary rather than by their date of first or subsequent publication, thus focusing on Mary's apprehension of them rather than on the history of events, ideas or literature. Quotations from other diaries and extraneous material are also given in italics.

In some chapters, quotations are predominantly from Mary's diary; in others, especially Chapters 3, 4 and 6, they are predominantly from her reading texts, illustrating the material to which Mary's chosen reading exposed her, even though her responses are not always expressed in detail. This aims to provide a balance and interaction between Mary's voice and the many voices within her intellectual and cultural environment.

Forms of punctuation have been modernised to some extent; also contractions, familiar at this period, have not always been replicated. Punctuation and capitalisation in the diary script have occasionally been modified to fit grammatically into the narrative here, hopefully with no distortion of meaning. Mary's standard of literacy was very high, though handwriting is variable and not always easy to decipher, especially in childhood; in spite of every effort to avoid misreadings, these may have occurred in isolated instances.

Recent boundary changes between Cambridgeshire and Huntingdonshire have resulted in some apparent anomalies and some references to Huntingdonshire might now be only historically correct.

Chapter 1 of this book explores Mary and her diary, following both the timeline and features of her life, and includes also some historical/theoretical background. It attempts to begin to answer the question, "Who was Mary?". Chapter 2 discusses Mary's reading in a broad range of subjects. Chapters 3 and 4 focus on Mary's reading in religion, the most notable topic, perhaps, both of the era and of Mary's life; Chapter 3 devotes itself to the literature which supported Mary's view of religion and Chapter 4 to that which challenged it, although it is acknowledged that the distinctions here can be blurred. Chapter 5 focuses on gardens and wilderness, and contextualises them within Mary's life and her mental and spiritual activity. Chapter 6 positions

Mary in relation to the current conceptions of woman's role and to feminism and all their manifestations, both in what she read and how she lived. Chapter 7 also takes a distinct theme which emerges from Mary's experience of life, that of 'suffocation.'

I

Who Was Mary?

> But see to it, my friends, amid all your earthly blessings and enjoyments, that you do not set your whole heart on them; that you lay up your treasure elsewhere.
> (Boyd, *The Graver Thoughts of a Country Parson*, 2nd Series, 1865) p.261. (6/2.8.1863)

> The air quite soft & nightingales answering each other in the Long Walk.
> *Mary's Diaries* (16/11.5.1893)

The advice from Andrew Boyd reflects a state of heart and mind which characterised Mary all her life. The second, somewhat poetical quote, drawn from Mary's diary, close to the end of her life, is reminiscent of an entry from her childhood: **We all walked with Mama in the garden after her return. It was a lovely evening and the nightingales sang sweetly.** (23.5.1835). It represents Mary's conception of utopia which her beautiful gardens could provide for her -a balmy atmosphere and all creation at peace. It echoes, also, a happy observation upon natural harmony, which she made some years earlier: **Was amused with seeing the fox and 'Windsor' the fox hound puppy playing together on the lawn.** (13/4.8.1883). This idyll which she experienced on occasions in her garden and in the country, eluded her increasingly through her latter years, though she came to accept that, in the interests of her spiritual development, God would send chastisements, and she had not yet arrived in heaven.

Mary was of semi-aristocratic birth, born on 30th April 1822. Her mother, the Countess of Lindsey, was daughter of the Very Rev. Charles Peter Layard and widow of the 9th Earl of Lindsey, and her second husband, father of Mary and Elizabeth, was Rev. Peter William Pegus, an Anglican clergyman of somewhat lower social status than her first. Mary's Christian names are Maria Antoinetta, but these names also appear variously as Marie and Antoinette. On marriage, she took the surname Gordon, and when her husband acceded to the title of 10th Marquis of Huntly in 1853, she became Marchioness of Huntly. In fact, throughout her life, at least by family and friends, she was simply called Mary, a name which accorded well with a simple religious nature.

With her parents, younger sister Elizabeth, half-sister Charlotte (ten years older), daughter of the 9th Earl of Lindsey, and her half-brothers and sons of the Earl- Lindsey, the mentally challenged heir to the Lindsey title, and Bertie, an intellectually bright but somewhat incommunicative character, she spent her childhood at Uffington House in Lincolnshire, the ancestral home of the Earls of Lindsey. Despite the tempestuous character of her father, Peter Pegus, the depression and invalidism of her mother and the frequent difficulties of home life, she spent a generally happy childhood, enjoying the extensive gardens and surrounding countryside at Uffington and the company of the younger members of the household.

Mary's character was, in most respects, consistent through life. She hated the fashionable social round in which they were often obliged to participate and nearly always preferred to remain at home and enjoy her gardens. For younger half-sister, Elizabeth, even the visitors who arrived at Uffington were mostly superfluous to requirements: *"I think company is the greatest boar* (sic) *under the sun they always call when they are not wanted ..."* (*Elizabeth's Diary*) (8.3.1837). One year, Mary expressed herself *so* **pleased because we were not going to London this year,** asking **Who could leave the country when it is so beautiful as this?** (4.5.1834). She professed an unusually vehement dislike of the amusements provided for girls of her class, events which others might have much enjoyed or, at least, made the best of.

She reported on one occasion close to her marriage:

A dissipated week has intervened and left one with a long arear of Journal and a bewildering recollection of balls & parties of which the most pleasing reflection just now is that they are over, & that their history may be more speedily over, to return at once. (13.5.1843)

After marriage, there was some continuation of this. *Talked about fashionable society as it is in London which H.L. & I agreed in condemning. Will another generation improve upon it?* (2/20.11.1851); *Very headachy after the last day or two of dissipation.* (2/1.9.1852). Mary persisted strongly in this aversion throughout her life. She loved the unspoiled country, was strongly protective towards it, and reacted with horror to the mechanical workings and environmental destruction of the ironworks in Dowlais, South Wales, where she went, before her marriage, to visit the now-married Charlotte whose husband, John Guest, was the owner of the works.

Mary had always loved to be light-hearted and playful. She was spontaneously generous, although also acting in the tradition of the country house as the centre of local munificence. She wrote one day at the age of 14, *On our way saw the Cuttle village girls who asked permission to pick violets in the park which was immediately granted them.*(10.4.1836). Flowers were a common currency, and the facility both to pick and exchange established a form of pseudo-egalitarianism in which Mary found refuge. The child-like spirit continued and Mary would later enjoy the company of her own children and join them in their games and in caring for their pets. Even at sixteen, despite a recent tragedy soon to be recounted, she relished the company of younger children, describing how *every minute I can spare from home is spent with the dear children- The Layards are constant guests at dinners and a shoal of young ones generally pour in in the evening.*(15.10.1838). Somewhat later, at an age when most girls were thinking ahead to marriage, it had clearly seemed improper to Mary's mother that her daughter should spend her days playing with children. *Gave me a lecture at luncheon partly concerning the little girls whom I must give up.* (27.9.1842)

The playful Mary also had a very serious side. Home-educated like many girls of her class, she soon acquired a high standard of literacy, as demonstrated in the almost faultless writings in her diary, and she read widely and in depth, using the services of the circulating library. Her comments on books at an early age demonstrate a mature appreciation. At age fifteen, she wrote, *Miss Williams read aloud to me Scott's 'Highland Widow,' a very pathetic tale & related with great force* (1.11.1837). In 1839, at 17, she commented in notably acid tones on *The Idler in Italy* by Lady Blessington:

> *Excessively entertaining. It is astonishing how she can express the moral and religious sentiments she does when her conduct bespeaks her wanting in both- the recollection of this takes off very much from the interest I should otherwise feel in the perusal of her work.* (4.10.1839)

Such comments portray her as a feisty, somewhat opinionated, girl who, after her marriage, would appear to fade a little into the background, as she sank herself into the duties of wife, mother and marchioness, although it might be guessed that the assertive young person would remain intact somewhere inside herself. Description of her early reading is given in Chapter 2.

The first really devastating blow Mary suffered was the accidental death of her sister and chief playmate, Elizabeth, in 1837, from drowning in a canal on the Uffington estate. After the accident, Mary wrote:

> *Feel it is my duty not to waste my time in useless tears but to try & give what comfort I can to those who are still left for us to love. And yet this task is hard ... She was almost like an only sister to me & assuredly only companion.* (8.4.1837)

She stoically proceeded with daily life in an effort to accept what she assumed to be the Will of God and to spare others the burden of her unhappiness. Her grief, however, resurfaced, more than a couple of years later, at the death of Tiny, the little dog who had been a constant companion to both girls, and she wrote:

Tiny's death touches a stronger chord of sympathy with our hearts than she could have done merely from her own merits. It is enough to remember that she had a place in the childish affections of one that's gone & we no longer grudge the tears which could fall to the memory of a dog. (4.11.1839)

Emotions also rose high in a poem, beginning: *Oh bring my sister back to me/ I cannot play alone,* which functions as a preface to the volume of her diary beginning 15th October 1840. All sorts of feelings, conscious and unconscious, may have arisen in this context, including survivor's guilt, stronger, perhaps, because Mary was the elder sister of the two and was close by when Elizabeth drowned, but, beyond her basic cries of grief, she did not give expression to these more complex feelings, citing only the Will of God and her speculations on Elizabeth's resurrection to Heaven.

Following Elizabeth's death, Mary entered into a more sober and troubled adolescent life, as she was pressed to prepare for adulthood and marriage. She reported several humiliations and instances of reprimand from others. Whilst this is not unusual for a young person at this period, these episodes seemed to dominate her self-image, and she recounted the following instances:

I was miserably puzzled to discover a method to put things right again particularly as my efforts appeared only to draw down increased displeasure (after upsetting a servant). (7.12.1842)

C. came up to my room after I was in bed & talked much upon the subject of the expressed dissatisfactions with me. Being late at night all that was said affected me keenly and made me give way very foolishly. Char kindly sat up with me some time. (8.1.1843)

Mr Layard called & took luncheon & followed me upstairs to ask me very seriously why I had such a long bluedevilyface & adding that it was "a shocking thing to see such a beautiful young woman pining away." I spanned my waist quite alarmed and asked whether I really had grown so thin- all the time having a headache that might well stretch my fair visage beyond its natural limits. I grunted pretty savagely. (17.3.1843)

At one point, perhaps under pressure to conform to expectations, and expressing the angst typical of adolescence, she started to question her identity, asking, in response to criticisms of Sir John Guest, Charlotte's husband, **whether poor Mary with a burden of such heavy sins could have one friend left to say- "With all her faults, I love her well,"** (5.5.1843), and adding the following day in a fit of rebellion, **I feel a great contempt for all the world & still more for what the world says.** (6.5.1843)

A few weeks later her mood seemed to have worsened:

> *A sort of weight & depression had been gradually creeping on me & increasing at the termination of each morning's duties* (Mary then had a fit of exhaustion and fell asleep) *I could not have slept long before I woke in a state of suffocation- struggling hard for breath, I was glad when it was over and no one had seen me.* (24.7.1843)

'Suffocation' can be construed as a theme in Mary's life and will be the topic of the final chapter.

Mary had commented sympathetically on reading Fanny Burney's diary, *It is quite painful to find poor Miss Burney with her energies stinted & her genius fettered by the trammels of servitude & court etiquette,* (27.2.1843) and it seems that, in contemplation of adulthood, she was resentful of the possibility she, herself, might have to conform to a preordained role. A climax was soon reached. *I never felt myself so nearly on the brink of annihilation.* (31.7.1843)

Perhaps the key to the peace that Mary craved was simple and strongly connected with her need for closeness to nature, a need which was apparent through life. A few months earlier she had written:

In the evening read a sweet little book, 'Our Wild Flowers' by T.A Swanley- & went to bed full of pleasant visions of banks of violets & meadows of cowslips which succeeded in diverting my attention from the pain of my throat & soon converted my waking dreams into sleeping ones. (8.4.1843)

Increasingly, the world made demands. Mary's life, that of a young semi-aristocrat girl, had already, to a degree, been set out for her. Early circumstances affect everyone in later life, but the gender and class restrictions existing at this period substantially narrowed the options. The expectation had been that she would make a good marriage, perhaps helping to run an estate and providing heirs. She was introduced to Lord Strathavon, thirty years her senior and previously married without children, heir to the title of 10th Marquis of Huntly and the two estates of Orton Manor in Huntingdonshire some miles from Uffington House, and Aboyne Castle in Aberdeenshire. Strath, as Mary called him, a fellow Christian, initially a Tory, but later a Liberal, also represented East Grinstead and Huntingdonshire in the House of Commons and served as Lord-Lieutenant of Aberdeenshire from 1861. He would inherit the estates and title in 1853 upon the death of his father.

Mary was reluctant to leave her childhood and the life at Uffington. On her first visit to her future husband's family, she felt overwhelmed and wrote *I felt abroad which I attributed partly to my being principally among strangers & partly to my having lived so long in a limited world of my own.* (24.10.1843). She was, however, won over by the charm and kindness of Lord Strathavon and by her first view of Orton: **No written record of this day is required to impress it on my memory.** (29.2.1844). They soon married, and shared a warm and companionable relationship for nineteen years until the death of the Marquis. Thus, for Mary, the expectation was fulfilled in a largely beneficial way.

Charlotte is remarkable for following a different, somewhat less predictable course, one which Mary, alongside others, viewed as scandalous. She initially married John Guest, though he was owner of an ironworks in Wales, not a landowner or aristocrat. She had a large family but, after John's death, she entered into another, much more controversial marriage, this time with her son's tutor, Charles Schreiber, who was both younger than herself and her social inferior. During her life, she transgressed various boundaries, so that, as an extremely strong and independent character, she escaped many of the dictates of her destiny.

After her wedding, Mary found many aspects of her new life appealing, especially Orton's beautiful gardens. But, although the marriage was an affectionate one and the early years with Strath seemed to be happy, they were somewhat marred by her lack of confidence, which was a little at odds with the assertiveness which she had often demonstrated in adolescence, at least in terms of the attitude manifest in her diary. This was compounded by the age difference, but also persisted through her life and is explored below.

All too soon there came news that the estate was in trouble and, in due course, problems began to multiply:

> At 6. after S. had returned from Peterboro' walked with him down the Long Walk feeling much distressed in mind. ... poor dear S. said at dinner everything went against him & I made up my mind I must be more cheerful but with prospect of having to take Miss E's duties upon myself with little strength to fulfil them it is not easy. (2/11.6.1853)

Charles Gordon, her son, the 11th Marquis, later gave some commentary on this in his autobiographical works, referring to his grandfather the 9th Marquis, but also to the general problems that many estates were undergoing at this time.

> "Unfortunately, in the year 1824 he was one of the victims of the banker Fauntleroy, who ruined so many prominent people. Most of his estates were strictly entailed, and came under the management of trustees; owing to his advanced age, the timber had to be depleted without much consideration. The estates of Glen Quoich and Glen Garry, in Inverness-shire, and of Corrachree and Balfour, in Aberdeenshire, which were not entailed, were sold by the trustees."

> "The ordinary passer-by criticises the break up of a large estate without knowing the causes that led to it. There is generally appalling ignorance respecting agricultural and estate affairs among the mass of English men and women. They see broad acres, but know nothing of the cost incurred in cultivating them, of the heavy

burdens in rates and taxes upon them, and dismiss the matter with the hackneyed phrase that "All landowners and farmers are inveterate grumblers."

Soon, Strath's already declining health took a clear turn for the worse and Mary had to watch him approaching death and finally, after a long period of illness, nineteen years into the marriage, dying without even the comfort that the family heritage was safe. In the meantime, two babies died in infancy- not unusual for the period but, nonetheless, very distressing to Mary. After his death, she missed her husband deeply and kept feeling that he should be participating in all that was taking place. *It seems cruel to enjoy this place without him.* (7/25.10.1865)

She was left to cope with two large, now heavily compromised estates, and twelve surviving children. These in order of birth were Mary, Evelyn (Evy), Charles (heir to the estate, later called Aboyne, subsequently Huntly), Lewis (Lewie), Bertrand, Douglas, Esmé (Esmae), Grace (Gracie), Granville (Grannie), Margaret (Maggie), Elena (Nellie), Ethelreda (Ethel). The children brought mixed blessings. In the early years, the older boys could be boisterous and difficult to handle. In later years, she had to pursue careers for them, and sent Bertrand to Australia and Lewie into the navy. Both died abroad. The eldest boy, Charles, now called Huntly, rumoured to be an inveterate gambler, lived a long life and developed socialist views. He served under Gladstone and became Father of The House of Lords in 1930. Mary's relationship with him could be an uneasy one at times: **Spoke to Huntly about plans- he got so cross he made me ill.** (8/14.9.1867). Esmé met with serious financial difficulties and was made bankrupt in 1891. Bertrand, Lewie and Douglas suffered early deaths. For the girls, there was concern for marriage partners, prospects and settlements. Maggie, much to her dismay, had to take a much diminished settlement, since resources were rapidly running out. Evy and Gracie and the three younger girls joined the men on the hunting field and Gracie, consequently, had a serious accident. Mary once complained in her diary: **Nellie hurt- very miserable about all this hunting and hunting accidents.** (13/ 11.1.1884). There were, as usual, presentations at court to attend, the London season- all the paraphernalia of worldly climbing and sociability. Mary received loyal support from her children but, although in favour of women's suffrage, she was not a great follower of feminism, possibly not feeling the need, and did not identify with the political activities of some of her girls and those of their generation.

Above all, there was a deteriorating financial situation and, despite the participation of lawyers, advisors and relatives, the estates, alongside a large number of others, gradually became insolvent. Mary soon came to realise that her family were not the only landowners currently experiencing difficulties:

> *Walked to the old garden wall with Mr. Stephen and told him of the difficulties that had arisen as to management here. He said that things of the same kind had occurred on the Estate of Mr. Campbell of Blitheswood.* (7/20.8.1864)

Thus a personal tragedy was gradually apprehended as a wider social issue, but this only provided limited comfort. Acres of land at Aboyne were sold, and Orton Hall was rented out for a period, although Mary was able to reoccupy it and stay there till she died, despite the dismal mention some years earlier of the *prospects of a forced sale of the Orton estates*. (14/20.9.1886). One of the hardest things for Mary was receiving blame: ***Did not sleep being anxious & knowing that the children attribute the want of funds to mismanagement upon my part***. (12/7.4.1881); and, following a letter from Amy, Huntly's wife, ***He*** (Huntly) ***poor fellow thinks we have mismanaged things for him***. (12/14.1.1882). The downward trajectory of Mary's life in the period before Strath's death, and for many years after, occupies the bulk of the latter part of her diary, forming a sombre and ever-darkening sequel to an account which began with the spontaneous happiness of a child delighting in simple things, the natural world and the people around her and continued with a promising marriage and the much-welcomed births of fourteen children (twelve surviving infancy).

Distinguishing this, especially from the preceding period of history, was the slow decline of agriculture, accelerating towards the end of the century, and of the landed lifestyle, involving economic depression, climate change, poor harvests, and the prospering of industry. Awareness of this was generally slow, but the eventual realisation was graphically presented in a report in *The Times* on an agricultural conference in 1892:

> "There was very little talk of depression 18 months ago; we

all thought we had turned the corner and begun a new era. The majority of farmers were making a fair living, and we were looking forward to brighter times. These hopes have been ruthlessly dispelled, but may we not hope that better seasons will restore the balance?"

All the years following Strath's death were overshadowed by the battle to keep the estates intact and within the family- a battle that was all but lost by the time Mary died, when Aboyne Castle had been sold and the Orton Estate was threatened with the same fate. Not only was there loss of land, but there was the constant need for economies, which was stressful. Amongst all this there were deaths, Bertrand, Mary's third son in Australia, from a tropical disease, Lewie aboard a sunken naval ship, Douglas from chest problems following a series of riding accidents. Mary had also lost two babies, Randolph and Edith (Nellie's twin). Her parents had died and her servants and some of her children were out of control. Some of her friends eventually turned against her: **Lady Westmoreland passed us as we were walking back & I was rather amused by the line she is taking in not speaking to the family.** (13/2.6.1883)

There were many very low points: **Walked round the wilderness with Davy, feeling ill & burdened.** (6/11.10.1863); **Couldn't sleep from thinking what has to be done** (12/22.6.1881); **Most of the family were dancing at Orton a year ago! May all trials sent by God work together for our good.** (14/31.12.1885); **Very low both about Aboyne and Orton** (14/12.7.1887); **Sickening letters from Robertson and Hurry** (14/15.7.1887); **About the sale of Aboyne- Tears would come as I wrote.** (14/29.7.1887). She became substantially disillusioned with the world, as her difficulties and her pain progressed, and she lost both people and assets that were dear to her.

Mary, whilst capable of independent thought, was not the stuff of which rebels are made. Unconventional as she was in some of her attitudes, nonetheless, in family matters, she remained dutiful. As a young person, she was capable of sulking but would soon, under the influence of religion and her own accommodating nature, become compliant and, indeed, the conformist and 'passive' part of Mary was, on the whole, productive of happiness while the good things lasted, though she was prone to ailments such as headaches and sore throats, many of which were probably of a psychosomatic nature, suggesting that subconsciously the conformity came at a cost. She did not have much resilience to cope with the deteriorating situation, though duty ensured her perseverance in the interests of her children and the family heritage: She wrote:

> *Mr. Bircham called upon me from Mr. Brooks wishing that I should make some arrangement to give up Orton- I told him what I have felt from the beginning that I might give it up temporarily but that I could not in justice to the children deprive them permanently of a home.* (8/ 4.6.1869)

Mary's struggles with her social and economic destiny cast her often as unequal to the task and ultimately some kind of 'failure,' but the odds were generally heaped against her and these were not the circumstances in which she could shine, so it is rewarding to look more deeply into her character. Firstly, whilst avoiding the noisy and crowded venues, Mary was capable of deep and warm relationships. Many were based on a shared passion for botany and gardening, but also there were friendships with authors, such as Anthony Trollope who visited a number of times, and clerics, most notably Charles Kingsley. G H. Marsh was a friend from childhood who had taken holy orders and was also very knowledgeable in botany, and neighbours. Tenants and children on the estate were also often her friends. She was, with few exceptions, very sensitive to the needs of others; on the visit of a family friend who had recently lost his wife, she was able, even as a 17-year old girl, to comment with sympathy: *Mr. Edmunds was walking about the grounds when we reached home looking ill & out of spirits. Poor man he has found what a wilderness this world is without anything to love or care for in it.* (28.8.1839). She also very much appreciated kindness from others.

Towards her own children Mary was very tender: *Almost broke my heart* (leaving Baby Douglas to take a journey) (2/4.2.1852); *Went out in the morning & unfortunately forgot little Douglas who was to have gone with me. On my return from the Long Walk found him under a tree sobbing in despair at having lost me.* (3/14.3.1856). Later she had to mourn the early death of this much-loved son. Lewie, her third son was a somewhat wayward child but she was deeply upset when Strath administered physical punishment to him. When, as a young adult in the navy, he died in the sinking of his ship, HMS Captain, she was overwhelmed with grief. Huntly described how, at Huntly Lodge in Aboyne, on the night of September 6th-7th 1870, his mother had been *"disturbed in the night by seeing the apparition of my brother Lewis"* and was *"very much agitated."*

He continued to recount that:

> *"He appeared to her as lying on a couch and fast asleep; she tried to wake him but was unable to. So positive was she that he had appeared to her and something was wrong, that she declared her intention of communicating with the Admiralty to make enquiries."*

Mary, herself, wrote:

> **At 3pm Huntly came to bring some awful news that the Captain has foundered off Cape Finisterre. Early in the morning of the 7th. All have perished- my beloved & bold Lewie among them. God's will be done.** (9/10.9.1870)

Despite her generally sweet nature, Mary was not universally charitable, but had some blind spots and intolerances. For example, as seen earlier, she valued straightforwardness and transparency which facilitated trust and she admired loyalty to family and tradition. Somehow, at least in the early years, she found Charlotte too complex and unpredictable. A childhood entry illustrates her incredulity and impatience at Charlotte's unfathomable behaviour: *Letter from Charlotte to Mama. Planning a visit. Leaving Dowlais (yesterday) but for where- they were unable to tell. (as usual!)* (29.1.1835). Charlotte's second marriage to her son's tutor created mayhem in the family and she was condemned by Mary alongside the rest of the family: *Heard from Papa- deprecating the event alluded to in my letter. We talked over what steps could be taken to avert such a calamity & all agreed that it would be desirable for Mama to write.* (3/27.1.1855); *Met (?) who, as did many others attacked me about Charlotte.* (3/1.6.1855). Decades later, she was unable to resist quoting her daughter Nellie's remark that she was afraid of Charlotte because she was **so clever** and **looks at you like a piece of china.** (10/12.1.1877). Nonetheless Mary and Charlotte developed a close relationship through the years. Similarly, she had, in the early years, some problems with her half-brother's (Bertie's) wife, Felicia, who was prone to promise she would come to visit and then apparently change her mind.

She also had little time for royalty and its ceremonies:

Went to the Queen's ball alone (a great bore!) at 10 got home at 12. (3/1.6.1855)

To meet the Queen who is passing down the country today. Her Majesty was more gracious than usual in spite of the weather & asked for Aboyne & Lewie to be brought to the carriage to her. (3/15.10.1855)

Down to the Inn to see the Queen change horses on her way to Balmoral ... S. stood speaking to the Prince who was very gracious ... but the Queen I thought looked cross as usual. (3/30.8.1856)

She admired persistence and hardihood and disliked spoiltness and self-indulgence:

> *Read Dr Bowen's life- The account of his sojourn in Africa and the death of his wife is very touching. I felt his life to be a great & comforting example of perseverance.* (6/6.4.1863)

> *Finished reading Impressions of a Tenderfoot by Mrs Algernon St Maur. A very interesting account of the travels with her husband in search of game. Her cheerfulness through a rough life of fatigue & privation contrasts favourably with the moans of Lord Randolph Churchill from the Transvaal from which it appears that from a menu of about 30 dishes he can find nothing to eat.* (15/30.7.1891)

Despite these blind spots, Mary's overriding quality was that of compassion and this is shown clearly in her warm friendship with half-brother Lindsey, someone to whom she found plenty to give, with little obviously to gain. As the mentally challenged heir to the Lindsey title, Mary, in gentle humour, called him 'My Lord,' and was tolerant of his eccentricities. She played with him in childhood and retained her warm feelings towards him until his early death.

Beyond particular friends and individuals, Mary had a fund

of compassion for all people and animals who were suffering or in need- something which was heartfelt and quite distinct from her general philanthropic efforts. Note her internal agonisings on visiting a man dying of consumption in a cottage, during a visit to see Charlotte in Wales, after the marriage of the latter to ironmaster, John Guest: *The subject of 'prayer' was brought up at dessert, with it so many serious thoughts in my heart. And I went upstairs & wept bitterly.*(12.8.1843). She spoke with similar feeling of a neighbour who was dying in pain: *To see her suffering quite alone day & night & yet lying so patiently. I could not bear to leave that poor creature suffering there and not find it in my power to help her.* (28.9.1843). She recounted industrial accidents, clearly with the sense that new technology could be inhuman in its application. Even as death approached her, she recorded a *serious agricultural accident.* (16/21.5.1893). Accidents in coalmines she found particularly upsetting, perhaps because they reminded her of the mines at Dowlais which had horrified her on her visit to see Charlotte at Dowlais.

Cruelty to animals distressed her greatly, though here she was conflicted, since her husband, some of her children and some of her friends and neighbours were avid hunters. However their behaviour might offend in this regard, her obvious disgust never found expression in reproach of her husband and she seemed to force herself to show support for his pleasure, writing: *S. went to the window to look at the prize* (deer?) *& spoke more like himself?'* (later eviscerated?) (3/24.7.1854); *'S. returned with a deer! We were all delighted as this is the last day of the season & he has been so unfortunate this year.*(4/14.10.1857). Later she mentioned *a capital* *days sport having killed more than 100 pheasants.* (4/11.12.1857). Her real feelings about abuse of animals appeared on many other occasions: **Was much discomfited on my return in interrupting great cruelty to a horse.** (1/28.8.1846); **Walked up the Long Walk- the children finding birds' nests & treating them happily with some tenderness.** (6/1.5.1864); **Garden boy, Bill Henson caught destroying nests.** (6/13.6.1864); **Stopping the murder of the old rooks on their nests.** (13/14.4.1884); **Cruelty to calf.** (10/20.9.1875); **Cruelty to a pony.** (13/17.10.1882); **Deplored the cruelty to animals in this country.** (14/18.4.1888)

Mary seems to have been generally well liked by those who knew her well. Huntly, Mary's eldest son, spoke warmly of her in his autobiography, *Milestones*, and gave a beguiling picture of her:

> "My mother was of medium height, with rather sloping shoulders, dark brown hair, regular features, and a lovely complexion. She was a strong advocate of out-of-door exercise, and was full of energy, even coming to bowl at cricket to me and my brothers when we were lads at school."

He stated that she was *"a strong Liberal and an advocate of the enfranchisement of women all her life."*

It seems, however, that, as life progressed, Mary felt herself often unable to fully meet its challenges. Because she found it difficult to assert authority, she appears unnecessarily self-deprecating. Immediately following her wedding, this deficit of confidence, with an admixture of gender modesty, prompted the following humorous entry:

> *I did not feel the least bit of a heroine, or gain any additional importance from the fact of its being my wedding day- a laughing fit occasioned by having the term 'my lady' applied to myself, made my exit alone with my 'lord and master.'* (1/9.4.1844)

A few days later she delineated her new role in words that might seem strange for a woman of her class, maybe even a little tongue in cheek: *I am now about to take upon myself some of the important duties of a housewife in arranging the rooms &c. Success attend my first attempt!* (1/15.4.1844). The coyness about her newly acquired status continued: *Poor Mr. E said Lady Aboyne with a great effort but still persisted in doing so in the face of my protestations against it.* (1/20.8.1844)

Mary described her relationship with Strath in the early years: *I rejoice in his opinions on many subjects which hitherto I have only longed to meet with hear expressed.* (1/18.4.1844); *Proffered my humble assistance.* (1/19.4.1844). She resolved to refrain: *from ever loving any earthly thing better than my husband and my home, but that still subordinate to my love to God, and my hopes of a better home eternal in the heavens.* (1/23.4.1844). She was unsure, however, how to adapt her behaviour to her awesome new responsibilities as wife to a Lord: *The office of reading the Sermon & prayers to the servants was deputed to me & I executed it as well as I could, tho' impeded by a little nervousness.* (1/19.5.1844). *Did some* shopping with Strath in the afternoon ... I was afraid of saying too much or too little, though I most probably erred in doing the former. (1/25.9.1846).

A few years after marriage, Mary seemed to go through one of her depressive episodes, feeling even her anxiety to be sinful:

> In the afternoon- sent for Dr. Hopkinson who told me I grew ill & thin because I was not more cheerful, & threatened me with Madeira if I did not look more smiling- which I thought rather arbitrary. However I believe- I am often over anxious- & as this is inconsistent with the peace & confidence that religious principle can alone inspire. I must do my best by attention to all physical & mental causes of irritation, to overcome it. (1/8.12.1848)

Her relationship with her much older husband would remain subservient, although probably more from her own instigation than his; indeed, he was far from unkind or tyrannical. Mary acknowledged how her nervousness sometimes irritated him, as on one occasion when she was phased by his unexpected entrance: *S came in rather suddenly which made me hysterical & annoyed him.* (2/19.11.1851); *Feeling weak & dispirited. ... S. was displeased with me, & I felt very low. Went to bed very unhappy.* (2/3.2.1852). Similarly, she had difficulty on social occasions, as when she *accompanied S. to Charlotte's ball ... My diamonds tumbled on my nose & I was glad to get home.* (2/14.5.1851)

Major problems occurred in her relationship with servants and there are many references to this:

> *I had an accumulation of business and in addition to this, a screw loose* (?) *in the nursery arrangements which what from sorrow at leaving the children & not being well, I lost all power of putting right & could only sit down & cry.* (1/2.8.1847)
>
> *At home distressed at finding there had been kerfuffles among servants.* (1/5.10.1847)
>
> *Miss G lecturing her* (Mary Junior) *upon impatience and ingratitude ... Sat down by her bedside* (Mary had earache) *and felt quite overcome by the weight of so many anxieties ... found her* (Sarah, a maid) *greatly offended with me & quite implacable. I tried in vain to soften her & at length went down crying ... poor Baby.* (2/16.12.1851)
>
> *Went to bed feeling poorly & nervous.* (2/17.12.1851)

Once she expressed herself unable to cope with the domestic organisation for a visit to Aboyne:

> *Disagreeable domestic arrangements & it is quite impossible to find exactly the accommodation that everyone requires. I felt quite oppressed with the numerous requirements & wished myself at Orton alone with baby for a fortnight leaving the members of the household to fight it out.* (3/5.7.1855)

Childcare staff also caused her problems: *Feverish & anxious about the change of governesses for the children at night.* (4/15.4.1857)

In March 1858, she reported servant issues keeping her awake. Later she had to cope with Smith, a particularly intransigent senior servant:

> *Smith came up in the morning- went through his day book with a view to arriving at an idea of the produce of the Farm He was very tiresome doing all he could to mystify instead of elucidate. My day was all spent in this agreeable manner- with very little in the way of good results to show for it.* (5/21.11.1861)

Mary never quite outgrew her nervousness in her interactions with her household. A classic example of her timid approach and an illustration of its lifelong nature occurred when, the year before her death, Mary delegated to her son-in-law the task of reprimanding a servant:

> *The former* (George, Nellie's husband) *kindly again interviewed Cook & told him of my being aware of how badly he has been going on & that on the next cause for complaint he would have to leave.* (15/22.1.1892)

Mary could be ill at ease, both with the glib entitlement

of the upper classes of which she was a member, but also with the rougher manners sometimes manifest within the lower classes and this conflict of feelings contributed to these difficulties with servants. Sadly it was partly because of her gentle nature, construed, perhaps as timidity, that Mary was so greatly taken advantage of by servants, who tended, as it seemed, to lack respect for her. And yet almost everything she had to deal with, including the marriages of her children, seemed to evoke this nervousness in her: *Lady Caroline Turnor proposing her son Edmund for dear Mary* (Mary Junior). *This fills me full of anxiety & perplexity.* (7/2.2.1866)

Sometimes Mary seemed to be caught in contradictory requirements, for example the demand of her husband that she play a full role in running the estates alongside the need not to appear inquisitive beyond a certain point, ironic in view of her later necessary involvement in the attempts to salvage the estates after Strath's death: *S. gave me a lecture for looking too much into the affairs & in my zeal not sufficiently considering the feelings of others. Thought about it in the night & did not sleep well.* (2/30.11.1852)

Why did Mary write her diary? She began it in 1832 at the age of ten, in imitation of Charlotte who had also started her pocketbook in 1822, at a similar age. Diary-keeping was a well-established practice among some middle- and upper-class women, but more is needed to account for why she continued to write her diary so faithfully. It is difficult to know for whom she wrote, other than for her future self or as a contribution to her spiritual journey. Did Mary want her children to read her words, and was there, as sometimes seems, a motive of constant self-justification? As she approached death, she appeared a little vague about the future of the diaries, consistent perhaps with her generally low estimate of her own importance. She showed little concern as to whether her journal was publicised or even whether it survived, apparently leaving the decisions to her eldest daughter: **Mary** (Junior) *asked me who should have charge of my journals at my death to keep or destroy as they might think well & I suggested herself.* (15/23.11.1889). In fact, it was ultimately as part of her daughter Ethel's papers (the Wickham (Cotterstock) collection), that Mary's childhood diaries finally found their way into Northamptonshire Record Office where they remain today. After the seemingly brief exchange with her eldest daughter, Mary focused on other less momentous topics, including Mary (Junior's) arrangements for getting home by train. This apparent disinterest in the future of her diaries could be partly accounted for by the fact that she had written comparatively little that was acrimonious about others, most of her aggression having been turned against herself, or it might be that she held her life and achievements in low esteem but, confident that she had tried to be a good Christian, was now focused on the life to come.

There is another reason for her persistence in diary-keeping, upon which an entry made a few months before her marriage may shed some light. Here, after apologising for missing some entries, she wrote, apparently addressing herself:

I know you will say some day 'The records of those days have a deep interest for me' for although events were then monotonous they had a dayspring of life in them... I shall seek in those pages many a clue to the causes (however trivial in themselves & slightly defined) of those impressions which I might otherwise have indulged/exercised my retrospective spirit in again to discover. (15/10/1843)

Thus, it seems, she was writing for herself, not only to record events, but to be able at a later date to make valid links between the past and later times though, if these were the sole motivations, she would have seen no reason for her diaries to survive her and would possibly even wanted them to be destroyed.

Clearly she had some sense that her diary could be of value after her death, but preferred that her children should award her that value, rather than she should claim it for herself, just as she had refrained from seeking undue publicity for some of her other achievements. Yet, also the diaries, whilst a record of events and feelings, drew on an earlier tradition in which the dynamic was the continuous process of spiritual self-improvement, and the impression is here reinforced by Mary's tendency to assess her progress on her birthday or at the transition to new year. Her daily entries are not only retrospective, stating what has happened (with little looking forward except, in a religious spirit, to heaven), but are also justificatory in that she has endeavoured to follow a path of duty, 'ticking off' the list of things that were done of necessity, whilst admitting shortcomings. We cannot know entirely and the answers may have lain deep in Mary's subconscious.

Although there are some gaps in the records, mostly during the turmoils of adolescence when her enthusiasm for keeping a diary waned, or events made this difficult, or in her childbearing years when the demands of motherhood were overwhelming, she always returned to it with renewed commitment. Typical of a Victorian diary is the omission of any discussion of sex and physical details of childbirth; also, notably absent in later volumes are references to the early tragic death of her sister at Uffington, although this had affected her so deeply at the time, suggesting a lot of suppressed emotion as well as a mature decision to move on with her life. She rarely dramatized herself but saw herself in relation to the dramas of those around her, Charlotte's marriages, scandals and achievements, Lindsey's struggles and misfortunes, her father's volatile behaviour, the fame of the Layards (her mother's family) the cruelties to people and animals, and all that affected her husband, children and grandchildren. Herself, she presented, sometimes happy, sometimes unhappy, occasionally angry, rarely forceful, but usually as a well-intentioned person doing her best, though not always able to cope. Her account is primarily ordered by the clock, for her days were punctuated in Victorian fashion and in an especially gendered way, by meals, religious rituals, social events and so on, activities often disconnected from each other; she referred to her intention of ***dividing the day into regular hours for my various occupations- leaving half an hour in the morning for Scripture reading with the children.*** (2/ 4.2.1852). In widowhood and as the children got older, her time tended to flow more freely, so that she could, for example, spend all day reading or gardening or even travelling.

There is a strong sense of place and the associated positives of home and garden. Uffington and Orton and Aboyne were the home sites, with other homes and gardens visited by Mary presented as alternatives for comparison. Occasional trips to Europe were documented. Rural conservative life was a norm for Mary, with urban and industrial locations presented as the sites of forays, often of an undesirable nature, a particularly discordant note occurring on Mary's trip to the mines at Dowlais, as related in the final chapter. Whilst admiring the aesthetics and grandeur of great houses, Mary was normally more impressed by their degree of homeliness and comfort for families:

> *In the afternoon we drove to see the farfamed Harlaxton. The house but more especially the internal fittings & decorations even surpassed my expectations. It is difficult at first to realize the beauty & magnificence of the objects which meet your eye at every turn. There is something however gloomy in its very magnificence, still more so when associated with the builder & his heirs who have since come into possession of it.* (6/27.3.62)

The diary is an account of how Mary spent her days, incorporating a narrative of events and thoughts, comments, feelings and hopes. There is little that is subversive or rebellious against a patriarchal society. Inasmuch as there is protest, it is usually against fashionable society, frivolity, any form of cruelty to people or animals; also technological progress which she often saw as detrimental, as when she remarked in describing a social gathering, that everyone looked much older since electric light was not becoming. (15/15.5.1889). Like many others, she did, nonetheless, welcome the freedom to travel afforded by the new railways and some other modern conveniences. She was thankful for her blessings, the bounties of the natural world, her happy marriage, her children, the workings of Providence, and even the acts of chastisement by God, although contemplation of these could sometimes breed a fatalism which could enable her to evade any sense of direct responsibility for such misfortunes, as the misbehaviour of some of her children, the bleak fate of the family estates, the indiscipline of servants.

It is often said that a diary serves to make sense of life. Mary's diary doesn't really attempt to do this except by invoking Providence, chastisement and God's Will. This can make for spiritual sense though occasionally producing narrative boredom. Some unexpected cynicism occurs in a reference to **the real game provided by the circumstances of life** following Lady Turnor's proposition of her son Edward as husband for Mary Junior, and this seems out of character for the adult Mary, though reminiscent of many comments on people and events made by Mary in adolescence before she learned conformity to the world's ways. (7/2.2.1866). It reinforces Mary's notion of herself as sufferer, though she lacked the self-pity which would make it unpalatable.

Mary's diary was her friend whom she visited daily to make

an entry but to whom she also resorted to recall the past: *Read dear old journal and Vaughan's lectures on Revelations.* (7/5.11.1865); *Looked out my old journal books and read my notes on our trip to Tyrol and Switzerland in 1871.* (12/6.8.1882); *Got out my old journal books hoping to find description of Victoria's coronation.* (14/14.6.1887); *Made notes from foreign journal.* (14/12.2.1888). She wrote nearly every day of her life, but sometimes she made the entries for several days in one sitting. Sometimes she wrote a few lines, sometimes close to half a page or more. Illegibility is an occasional problem, and the text can sometimes benefit from magnification. She provided a narrative of her day, and was careful to give balanced coverage, but she usually emphasised family and matters of garden and wilderness and mentioned the discussions in which she had engaged, what she had read and any observance of religion. She showed clear reactions to many things, so that the reader is well aware of her feelings, problems and preoccupations. Her critique of books, whilst frequent, is often not detailed. The accounts run into detail primarily in the garden and countryside but also around family and religion.

Social duties, including attendance at Royal functions, were often written as a tedious list. When she made many visits she had to name them all, though without an enthusiastic or detailed description of each. A summary sentence or two would have avoided the boredom of reading the uninspired list. Thus, on occasion, this is a plodding narrative, often a recital of the performance of routine and duty, which can be self-justificatory, but it is thoroughly redeemed by:

a) the infectious enthusiasm expressed for all aspects of the natural world

b) the down-to-earth debunking of an overblown social world (Mary could be almost spiteful towards royalty.)

c) the charm of her, sometimes naïve ineptitude in facing so many challenging aspects of her life

d) her elevation of ordinary life

e) her failure to take herself seriously, so that, even through difficult times, her accounts can be leavened with humour

f) the extraordinary amount of her reading and the fact that much of it is recorded

g) her clear expressions of feeling towards her friends, family and those who suffered

h) her anger at those who were shallow, treacherous, cruel, destructive or obstructive, and sometimes at those she felt disloyal to family, including Charlotte at the time of her second marriage

i) her very faithful and sincere pursuit of her Christian religion

The diary entries are full of everyday concerns. Someone has called, the servants are quarrelling, the weather has been stormy, letters have been sent and received. Mary, though proud of her garden and botanical collections, never presented herself as heroic or accomplished, and seemed to experience herself, somewhat passively, as akin to Alice in Wonderland; throughout her life, most things good or bad happened to a somewhat bewildered, though generally accepting self.

A diarist's perceptions of him/herself are unlikely to be exactly the same as the perceptions that others have of him/her. Fortunately, we have other accounts of Mary and her life which can be accessed for comparison. Some of these have been listed in the introductory chapter and referenced in this chapter. Mostly they are complimentary towards Mary and seem to find her innocent charm to be genuine.

Perhaps the best corrective to our perceptions of Mary are the reactions to her by others, some of which Mary, with her normal humility, herself records. They innclude the intolerance of family towards her sulkiness in adolescence, Strath's impatience with her inconfident handling of servants, the 'tactfulness' of the publishers to whom she submitted manuscripts. The saddest awareness, perhaps, is the realisation that, despite Mary's intelligence, she was widely patronised. This is partly in consequence of the gender discrimination widespread in her lifetime, and partly because of her own low self-esteem. She tended to internalise the more personal comments and to accept the generalised estimation of women's value. Chapter 6 focuses on these issues.

It would not be good to deny that, like most people, Mary had some degree of self-deception. Maybe a little of her dislike of attending glamorous social events was a reluctance to 'grow up' and assume the responsibilities of adulthood. Maybe when some of her children blamed her for the economic decline of the estates which should be their heritage- whilst this seems unfair in view of the forces set against her- her heart was not wholly in the efforts to fight, even though she did care about the consequences for the children. *(Conflict in my mind about the alienation of this place from the family.)* (13/1.7.1883). Note a comment made to her a little before the wedding of Mary (Junior): *Mr Watson dined with us and read prayers. Found fault with me for not coming out in the world and exerting myself more.* (7/15.4.1866). Then her condemnation of Charlotte's behaviour in flouting convention could contain some small element of jealousy of her half- sister's free spirit. Her comment, on first hearing of it, that she was **much shocked at this announcement**, sounds almost prudish, although familiarity with Mary's ways of thinking would consider that her care for the feelings of family made up the larger element. (1/4.1.1855)

I suggest that, despite postmodern denials of the existence of an authentic self or, at least, one accessible to the reader, the gardens, the books and the sincere religious devotion did all provide a touchstone of self. Both the inclination and the skills of self-presentation were largely absent in Mary. She didn't dramatize, idealise or rationalise. She revealed herself as 'trying' to do what was right according to her religion and the conventional expectations of a woman of her time; this involved the enjoyment of simple unworldly things and the endless performance of duty. The self-deprecating humour, which emerges periodically, confirms that she had no elevated image of herself to sell to any reader, as she laughed at herself on her wedding day and recounted her boredom and malfunctioning on social occasions.

In consideration of the 'socially constructed' self, evoked by the demands of conformity, and responsible for some fragmentation of personality, it could be seen that Mary, in particular, often resisted the process of social construction. She was required to occupy many roles, some sequentially, but most simultaneously. These include those of daughter, sister, wife, mother, hostess, political campaigner (on behalf of her son Douglas), aristocrat, estate administrator, philanthropist, botanist, gardener and socialite (a role she much detested). Willing as she was (though not always happy) to perform the duties of a Victorian woman of her class and, much as she valued her close friends and relatives, she never embraced the social role of an aristocratic woman. She used the gardens, the open country and books for her escape, and was strengthened by her Christianity.

2

The Books: Why? What? When? Where? How?

Books, regarded in their highest and truest light, are as much a part of nature as gardens. Gardens, indeed they are. We do not quit nature when from walking in the fields we step into our study; we only enter into another presence of nature.
(Grindon, *Life: Its Nature, Varieties & Phenomena* (s.n., 1856) pp.164-5. (3/11.11.56)

Mothers' meeting- All took away books with them to read at home ... They looked pleased and bright as if they liked it.
Mary's Diaries (14/18.11.1885)

The second quote here speaks for itself of the pleasure in books, often felt very keenly by those not accustomed to read them often. The first tells us that reading books and the study of the natural world are close allies. At this point the comparison is intuitive although, in Chapter 5, some of the actual similarities are suggested, in an analysis of Mary's reading and gardening.

It is well documented how reading in the nineteenth century increasingly made thought, information and observation much more widely accessible. It provided a shared experience and, at the same time, had some levelling effect, especially between upper and middle classes. To read became, not only fashionable, but an essential activity amongst those aspiring to some level of education and status, both filling leisure hours and enabling participation in civilised conversation. Increasingly this included women, though many never got beyond the region of light and entertaining literature epitomised by the novel.

Rev. Edward Bickersteth wrote:

> "*We live in a reading age, when education is almost universal, and men think and speak on all subjects with the utmost freedom.*" (Bickersteth, *The Works of Rev E. Bickersteth, 1832*) p.526. (*A Scripture Help*, London, s.n., 1852) (3/12.4.1854)

Mary's eldest son, Huntly, wrote early in the twentieth century in his autobiography, *Milestones*:

> "*Last century, with the introduction of railways, telegraphs,*

telephones, steam-boats etc. was an age of domestic revolution. The present century is an age of universal reading."

The social cohesion between the upper and middle classes was promoted by participation in a print culture and this was inclusive of many types of literature both fiction and non-fiction.

Undoubtedly, books and their borrowing, lending and discussion had become a form of daily currency, sustaining networks and linking friends, family members and cultural groups. Literature was no longer an elite study. Reading, indeed, became the measure of a person:

> "I am idleness itself, in spite of my early rising, as to everything but books; and though I do not study, I contrive to read some hours every day." (Trench, *The Remains of the Late Mrs. Richard Trench*, 1862) p.303. (6/25.9.1862)

> "If we may judge of people by the company they keep, we may try to judge of them by the books they read: and in this list, comparing the names with the volumes entered against them, it is interesting to watch how often the union throws an unexpected light upon the man, and how often it reveals him in a light completely new." (Liechtenstein, *Holland House*, 1874) vol 2, p.180. (9/ 3.12.1873)

> "The possession of many books bred a sense of cultivation and enrichment: next to pictures I am inclined to place

books." (Loftie, *A Plea for Art in the House*, 1876) p.71. (10/ 28.11.1876)

Reading was also a form of empowerment for the mass of people, especially within religion, where the clergy were no longer always the ultimate authority:

> "Spiritual reading has to a certain extent - more entirely for some minds than for others, but to a certain extent for all minds - taken the place of preaching: this has come about in the order of God's providence." (Goulburn, *Thoughts on Personal Religion*, 1864) p.109. (7/12.8.1866)

It was especially empowering for the upwardly mobile working classes and for disadvantaged groups such as prisoners:

> "Books, I thought, would tell me all I needed. But where to get the books?" (Kingsley, *Alton Locke*, 1887) p.21. (London: Macmillan, 1892). (14/ 15.2.1887)

> "One of the rules states that prisoners are not to exchange books with one another, but this was one of the few rules that I systematically infringed." (Thomson, *Five Years' Penal Servitude*, 1878) p.99. (11/4.3.1878)

Every individual woman would have had her own reading agenda. Mary was unusual in the scope and extent of her reading which was at the serious end of the spectrum, but tended to include what was recently published and currently fashionable at this level, and thus could be taken as fairly representative of a group of sophisticated readers, male and female. We know, for example that the novels of Charles Dickens were very popular:

> "Thousands were attracted to him because he placed them in the midst of scenes and characters with which they were already themselves acquainted; and thousands were reading him with no less avidity because he introduced them to passages of nature and life of which they before knew nothing, but of the truth of which their own habits and senses sufficed to assure them." (Forster, *The Life of Charles Dickens*, 1872) vol 1, p.125. (9/18.5.1872)

Accordingly, Mary (and her children) read many novels of Dickens; they also read numerous works of Sir Walter Scott, as Mary had herself done in childhood, and plenty of the works of Shakespeare.

To an extent, what was read was dominated by the circulating libraries which, following the decline of book clubs, had risen to prominence; in addition to a large quantity of novels, usually in the three volume format through most of the century, they supplied a range of good quality non-fiction on many subjects, all at an affordable cost. Mudie's, the most famous of them and the supplier of many of Mary's books, was committed to maintaining minimum standards of decency as accepted by mainstream middle-class culture, and there were a number of others including W. H. Smith, James Wilson, Jarrolds, Beaumont, Maggs Bros (for rare books and manuscripts), Day & Son, and Jarvis, all mentioned by Mary.

Library books found their way to various destinations; for example, philanthropy sometimes centred on providing literacy classes for young working men; also for prisoners and for members of the armed forces:

> "We have now lying before us an interesting document, a List of Religious and other Books for establishing a Library on board each of Her Majesty's Ships, for the use of the Crew" (Timpson, Memoirs of Mrs Elizabeth Fry, 1847) p.248. (1854) (1/6.3.1848)

These were also missions dear to Mary's heart and she devoted much time to the establishment of new, more accessible libraries: **Mr. & Mrs. Stackhouse called & I consulted them about a parish Library.** (1/13.4.1848); **Copied list of books for the Library.** (1/14.4.1848); **Directed shelves to be made for the village Library.** (1/23.11.1848); **Obtained a grant of £4 from the Xtian Knowledge Society for our Library. ... Prepared the library books ... to the School to arrange the books.** (1/24.11.1848); *I discussed with him* (Mr Ogg) *various plans of improvements for the people at Aboyne ... a long talk with Mr. & Mrs Jenkins about schools, a library, a reading room.* (2/4.10.1853); **Looked out books for a servant's library & read.** (2/11.10.1853); **Looked out books for the village library.** (3/8.10.1854); **Selected 12 books for the servants' library.** (3/19.10.1854); **Considered the subject of a village reading room** (3/16.12.1854); **Opening of reading room ... Benefit of reading among the labouring classes.** (3/

26.12.1854); *Called upon several of the people in the village & invited them to the reading room.* (4/31.10.1859); *The reading room to be open to young men- for mutual instruction.* (4/1.11.1859); *Set to work to empty the cupboards in the library and to place the books in the new book cases.* (4/30.11.1859); *Try & stimulate the young men into a mutual improvement Society.* (5/4.10.1860); *Read a good speech of Lord Stanley's on education among the lower order.* (5/31.10.1860); *Covered some books for lending out.* (6/13.8.1863)

Towards the end of her life Mary set up the Huntly Circulating Library: *Discussion with librarian on supply of books to rural districts & he is going to send me a list of the cheap and suitable books at their disposal.* (14/16.6.1886); *W.H. Smith offering £10 for the second hand books of which they have sent me a list to Mr Dack.* (14/21.6.1886); *Told Mrs. Hetley of my idea of a lending library for the rural population and we drew up an advertisement for the Peterborough paper.* (14/26.6.1886); *Wrote to Mr Dack about the advertisement of village circulating libraries.* (14/29.6.1886); *Mrs Hetley about the book scheme.* (14/12.7.1886); *Sent for Mrs Hetley who began classifying and numbering the books for 'the Huntly Library.'* (4/2.8.1886); *Mrs Hetley reported well of the progress of the Circulating Library.* (14/13.9.1886); *Talked to ... a schoolmaster about a supply of books from my Library.* (14/20.9.1886); *Mrs Hetley came about the library catalogue and she and Miss Perkins were at work all day posting in the rules. ... drove over to Normanton to take Mrs Brooks some library books.* (14/28.10.1886); *Mrs Hetley working with Miss Perkins on the books.* (14/29.10.1886); *Mrs Hetley binding and classifying the library books. Made some additions from the books sent from Tunbridge Wells.* (14/3.11.1886); *Mrs Hetley with a copy of* the catalogue of the 'Huntly Circulating Library'. For correction we added a book or two. (14/22.11.1886); *The Catalogue of the Library printed and given out.* (14/1.12.1886); *Mrs Hetley selecting books to allot.* (14/13.12.1886); *Harding quoted information he has received from the books of travel respecting conifers in their native countries and seems to appreciate the library and to find that others do so.* (14/2.1.1887); *Mrs Hetley came about addition of children's books to library.* (14/27.4.1887); *Wrote some of the biographical notices for the Catalogue.* (14/25.2.1888); *Sotheby's sale of books.* (14/30.5.1888); *Wrote asking for more books for the village libraries.* (15/4.10.18880); *Mr Heskett (?) sending me a Catalogue of a Village Library which he has instituted at Brough Yorks after the idea of mine.* (15/29.12.1888); *Looked through the books given by Ch G to the library taking out such as are not suitable.* (15/12.3.1889)

Mary was keen that a working man's newspaper be introduced. *Periodical newspaper is required for the education of the working men voters.* (15/23.11.1889); *Talked over a working man's newspaper & Mr Hake and I exchanged our ideas on the subject. He suggested the title of "The Voter" an improvement upon "The Householder."* (15/27.12.1889); *To Dean of Westminster about Working Man's Newspaper.* (15/29.12.1889)

Also she set up and spoke at Mothers' Meetings, making reading a regular part of the proceedings: **Read a little story about Linnaeus at the Mother's Meeting.** (15/7.3.1889); **Reading at the mother's meeting.** (15/13.2.1890). Her mission extended to individuals she knew: **Saw Harding** (her gardener) *& gave him a little book My Garden Wild to read.* (15/8.8.1892)

She looked at book reviews and often discussed books with family and friends: *Review of Dr Darwin's Book on the origin of Species in the Times.* (5/11.1.1860); *Talked over Novelists and Poets with Douglas.* (8/30.5.1870); *Talk with Mr. Holmes about Kingsley and the popular writings of the day.* (9/31.12.1872); *Some pleasant conversation about books.* (13/14.4.1883); *Spoke of Galton's book to (?) G. and he told me that he had had visions associated with figures, calculations, days of the week & co. which he had never thought worth mentioning before.* (14/4.11.1885); *Pamphlet giving the opinion of leading men and women as to which are 'The Best Hundred Books.'* (14/27.2.1886); *She told me of controversy now going on about Bacon's authorship of Shakespeare.* (14/23.4.1888); *Looked round the rockery & shewed Miss P the 30 Vols of Curtis Botanical Magazine purchased from Maggs which I had taken down with me.* (14/28.5.1888); *Read the much-talked of Robert Elsmere by Mrs Humphrey Ward which was reviewed in the spring by Gladstone.* (15/3.12.1888); *Granville came. Dinner with him- talked about books & essayists.* (15/19.12.1888); *Faithful & unfaithful turning upon the laws of divorce in the United States ... reviewed by Mr Gladstone.* (15/3.6.89); *Evy sends the Review of Reviews for July edited by W Stead Prince of Wales.* (15/8.8.1891); *In the afternoon pasted the correspondence from the Times on "The Bible and Modern Criticism" in a new book of newspaper cuttings.* (15/23.2.1892); *Professor Tyndale very interesting on Carlyle.* (15/2.5.1892)

There were many anxieties expressed by the clergy and others about the effects of 'light reading' especially for women. The theme of the mental stultification and blunted judgement, which could be induced by reading fiction, was a recurrent one, and there were prescriptions made by authorities in literature, the church and public life, of what kind of books should be read:

> "Shun as a plague, all works tending to excite sensual thoughts, or to defile the mind: they leave a polluting stain within, that will not easily be got rid of; they weaken the power of resistance against temptation; they often lead to total and final ruin." (Bickersteth, *The Works of, 1832*) p.161. (*A Scripture Help*, London, s.n. 1852). (16/6/1837)

> "And at the last day, be sure of it, we shall have to render an account- a strict account, of the books which we have read, and of the way in which we have obeyed what we read, just as if we had had so many prophets or angels sent to us. If, on the other hand, books are false and wicked, we ought to fear them as evil spirits loose among us." (Kingsley, *Twenty-five Village Sermons*, 1854) p.225. (1857). (3/14.1.1856)

> "The sort of deadness and exhaustion which I have often experienced, and seen in others, after reading novels." (Schimmelpenninck; Hankin, *Life of Mary Anne Schimmelpenninck*, 1860) p.109. (1858). (5/7.11.1860)

> "French novels. French romances, and French plays. The overflowings of that cup of excitement have reached our shores. Evil which comes in a form of grossness is not nearly so dangerous as that which comes veiled in gracefulness and sentiment. Subjects which are better not touched upon at all are

discussed, examined, and exhibited in all the most seductive forms of imagery." (Robertson, *Sermons*, 3rd series, 1857-9 *Sensual and Spiritual Excitement*) (Robertson, *Sermons Preached at Brighton, by the late Rev. Frederick W. Robertson*, New York: Harper, 1905) pp.514-515. (1860 onwards)

"Her brother Edward chose her books, and would not allow her to read novels." (Poel; Winkworth, *Life of Amelia Wilhelmina Sieveking*, 1863) p.20. (6/2.1.1864)

"And we strongly recommend to all young clergymen whose pulpit manner is not yet hopelessly formed, the reading of a good deal of light literature. They should read that to see what kind of matter interests the majority of minds." (Boyd, *The Commonplace Philosopher in Town and Country*, 1864) p.369. (6/9.5.1864)

"That wide class of readers, who only find in literature another variety of dissipation." (L'estrange, *The Literary Life of the Rev. W. Harness* etc., 1871) p.39. (9/11.3.1872)

"Interruption from the trash of book-clubs." (Hare, A., *Memorials of a Quiet Life*, 1872) vol 1, p.280. (9/21.8.1873)

"I have bought Gisborne's Duties of Women, Moore's Fables for the Female Sex, Mrs. King's Female Scripture Characters, and Fordyce's Sermons." (Macaulay; Trevelyan' *The Life and Letters of Lord Macaulay*, 1876) vol 1, p.353. (10/14.7.1876) (for his sister on her travels)

"No young person in these days should pick up books at haphazard. They should seek good advice as to what they read. The modesty of a life may wither in an hour." (Philpot, *A Pocket of Pebbles*, 1877) no.100. (10/3.3.1878)

"The object of a novel should be to instruct in morals while it amuses." (Trollope; *Thackeray*, 1879) p.109. (12/14.4.1880)

"But the novelist creeps in closer than the schoolmaster, closer than the father, closer almost than the mother." (Trollope; *Thackeray*, 1879) p.203. (12/14.4.1880)

"Novels ... regulate the views of life of hundreds and thousands of women, especially in the lower middle section of society, old and young. ... the mawkish and mistaken impressions of existence conveyed by the class of writings which these young women devour." (Escott, *England: Its People, Polity, and Pursuits*, 1880) p.532. (12/20.6.1880)

"There are outskirts on these regions, on which sweet-smelling flowers seem to grow, and grass to be green. It is in these border-lands that the danger lies." (Trollope; *An Autobiography*, 1883) vol 2, p.34. (13/25.2.1884)

"Look at our novels themselves, and see what sort of life it is they image- the trivial interests, the contemptible incidents, the absurdity of the virtuous characters, the viciousness of the *characters who are not absurd."* (Mallock, *The New Republic*, 1884) p.35. (1908) (14/28.12.1886)

"To the girls he was always courteous, asking their opinion, setting them right when they were wrong, lending them books, and directing them what to read." (Besant, *The Chaplain of the fleet*, 1887) p.8. (1891). (14/1.9.1887)

"Elizabeth looked down. She had never been allowed to read novels; but in the course of her nun-like existence she had read one or two nevertheless. If she had a sin indeed on her conscience, it was this; and an honest heart compelled her to make the confession." (Poynter, *The Failure of Elisabeth*, 1890) p.7. (New York: Lovell). (15/8.5.1891)

"There were literary young ladies, who had read everything of Dickens and Thackeray, and something at least of Sir Walter, and occasionally, perhaps, a French novel, which they better have let alone." (Holmes, *The Guardian Angel*. 1867) p.192. (Sampson Low, 1869) (15/8.6.1891)

"The result of much reading is the same as the result of no reading- the production of a blank." (Baring-Gould, *In the Roar of the Sea*, 1892) p.63. (New York: National Book Co., 1891). (16/20.11.1892)

Some 'improvements' in popular literature are noted towards the latter part of the century:

"The popular taste, thus cloyed with novels and poetry, turned to books on popular science, on statistics, on health, and on travel." (Besant, *Fifty Years Ago*, 1888) p.192. (15/14.3.1889)

Mary was well-connected to the intellectual world through her circle of family, friends and associates. Sir Austen Henry Layard, her uncle was an explorer of Nineveh and writer on this topic; novelist, Anthony Trollope, and cleric and novelist, Charles Kingsley were her friends; and her botanical associates, such as Miles Berkeley were often also writers. She moved in circles where contact with authors was not uncommon: **Introduced to Mr. Bradley Cuthbert Bede. (8/11.11.1867)**; **Thomasin Sharpe kindly presenting me with a book of which she is the author entitled A Royal Descent. (10/31.12.1875)**; **Mr Sutton Sharpe sending me a copy of the book he has published descriptive of Christ Church Cathedral Dublin. (19.1.1883)**. Professor Drummond, whose book *Natural Law in the Spiritual World* invoked uncharacteristic outrage in Mary, was in fact, also a friend. (See Chapter 4 for a discussion of her interactions with Drummond).

The why, when, where, how and what of Mary's reading are interconnected questions and inevitably due to a conflation of motivations and circumstances, but in studying Mary's reading practices, it is useful to analyse them separately. Starting with the 'why?' - Mary was brought up to read and she recorded a steady diet of reading in her early years. This became increasingly purposive until, at age 19, she resolved **upon a course of reading for the improvement of my mind being awakened to a ... sense** *of my own excessive ignorance* (2.9 1841). She was just as keen to record the books she read in childhood as those she read later; the problem is chiefly that of legibility for, in many cases, due to the fading of ink, the childishness of the writing and the lack of clarity and detail, what has been read cannot be ascertained. Even where a title or author is given, it is sometimes difficult to find publication details. Furthermore, those books read in earliest childhood before Mary had begun her diary have to remain obscure; gaps in the diaries and sporadic entries also have to be taken into account in reckoning the number and identity of her books. Nonetheless, it is clear that reading played a major role in Mary's family life and also that, alongside the lighter and more juvenile works, she had exposure to more demanding and more classical literature. Many of the books she read she also read at a later stage of life, sometimes to her own children.

Featuring heavily in childhood are novels of Walter Scott, sermons by various preachers, miscellaneous pieces by such poets as Gray, Milton, Byron and Southey, moral tales, historical, geographical, biographical and religious works. Southey's epic poem *Thalaba* in all its volumes was read aloud by Charlotte in early 1833 when Mary was only 10 years old, although she does not provide a reaction to this in her diary.

She read later to participate in the intellectual, fashionable and cultural life around her, to educate herself and her children and, especially, to find her way through the maze of controversy within the religious and scientific worlds. Like others, she also read for entertainment, citing a number of humorous volumes including, in childhood, Dickens' *Pickwick Papers* and *Martin Chuzzlewit* read in serialised form; also, in later years, Thackeray, *English Humourists*, 1800? (3/2.1.1854); Ward, *Artemus Ward*,1862. (6/10.2.1863); Black, *The Strange Adventures of a Phaeton*, 1872. (9/13.3.1873); Walford, *Mr. Smith: A Part of His Life*, 1875. (10/28.10.1875); Gillray; Rowlandson; Cruikshank; Bunbury; *Caricatures*,1830. (12/14.11.1880); Jessopp, *The Trials of a Country Parson*, 1890. (15/29.6.1890); Jerome, *Diary of a Pilgrimage*, 1891 (15/23.5.1891); Baring-Gould, *Historic Oddities and Strange Events*, 1891. (15/29.2.1892); A'Beckett; Abbott; Leech, *The Comic History of England*, 1893. (16/17.11.1892) She often described the less serious books, especially within fiction, as 'amusing', perhaps more with the meaning of entertaining than humorous.

Moving to the when and where, Mary read very regularly, most often in the evening, so the names of books tend to appear at the end of her diary entries, but the quantity of her reading increased as her life progressed and sometimes, at these later times, she would read all day, especially when there were fewer immediate demands from family. Priority was normally given to activities in gardening and botany, so she read particularly in bad weather, in winter and during periods of sickness and weakness. Towards the end of her life, when enfeebled with illness, she tended to read less demanding literature, such as novels. Most books she read soon after publication, especially where there was controversy surrounding them, but this was not to the exclusion of older works. She acquired books in response to the educational needs of children and servants. She also read books that followed on from previous reading or randomly, when recommended to read a book or given one as a gift, or on finding one in a library, or when information was required, or a particular need for comfort arose; the cleric, Frederick Robertson would be a typical choice in this latter situation. Sometimes she listened when someone else read aloud, a common practice at this time. She read, as many do, at home, in the bookroom or library or living room or garden, on train journeys and in vacations- with others, but mostly alone.

The question of how Mary read is particularly interesting as it touches on a philosophy of reading. There were varying views on the best ways of reading and this was of interest to Mary. She noted, **Felicia read aloud Sir James Stephen's lecture to the Young Men's Christian Association in September on systematic & desultory reading.** (3/17.9.1854)

Comments on the subject from authors were not infrequent:

"*Books must be read through from, end to end*" (Goulburn, *Thoughts on Personal Religion*, 1864) p.115. (7/12.8.1866)

"*He would steadily read for hours with the most perfect satisfaction, and never appeared to skip a single page.*" (Hare, A. *The Life and Letters of Frances Baroness Bunsen*, 1879) vol 1. p.25. (11/5.7.1879)

"*A book may be good for nothing; or there may be only one thing in it worth knowing; are we to read it all through?*" (Dr Johnson didn't want to read volumes about voyages).

"There can be little entertainment in such books; one set of Savages is like another." (Boswell, *The Life of Samuel Johnson*, 1862) vol 2, p.252. (Boswell's *Life of Johnson*, New York: Dutton, 1913). (14/9.5.1886)

Mary, herself, read at good speed, often finishing a substantial volume in one day, and rarely taking more than a few days, noting in her diary when she began and, often, when she finished. Whether she read every word cannot be known, but her persevering character and her own accounts in the diary suggest that, excepting reference works and those designed for occasional consultation, she did so in most cases. Usually her reading was a solitary occupation, but a substantial amount was read with her children, some with her servants or at mothers' meetings or other venues. Some was read aloud in interaction with other family members, and books were read to Mary when she was ill, especially at the end of life. A few books were read more than once and many repeats occurred in the context of her children's education as when, for example, the histories of Charles Knight and Thomas Macaulay were consulted in relation to disparate periods of history.

Moving finally to content; what Mary read may have been determined by many things:

1 By her time and opportunities for reading, varying through life, as well as her health, moods and differing capacities for 'serious' and light reading. For example, she engaged with a lot

of intellectually demanding texts following the death of her husband and resorted mostly to novels in her lengthy period of sickness preceding her death.

2 By what was topical or controversial or fashionable, since Mary was as subject to these influences as anyone else. Much of what she read was 'hot off the press' - sometimes even apparently in advance of its official date of publication. She referred, for example, to the **much-talked of Robert Elsmere.** (15/3.12.1888)

3 By the intellectual interests of the circles in which she moved and with whom she held discussion. There was much stimulation in daily life: *Meeting in the hall to hear Mr Miles explain some very ingenious illustrations he had made of the revolution of the earth round the sun- & of the length of day & night in different latitudes.* (3/22.2.1856); *Meeting one of the leading article writers for Times.* (13/7.11.1882)

4 By her own interests- generally broad, but concentrated in gardening, botany, religion and religious controversy, family books and books 'about people' (history, biography, travel journals etc)

5 By the current supplies available from the circulating libraries of which she used a number.

6 By linkage of authors and topics, for example, reading one book by an author, then another, frequent in the case of novels, but also true of non-fiction, for example, *Interesting little book*

entitled *Children of the World, a simple account of man in early times by Edward Clodd-* sought out another book by same author, *The Childhood of Religions* (11/4.2.1877); also by reading the works of a preacher or writer and later their biography as in the case of her favourite Frederick Robertson.

7 By educational needs of children, servants etc. In educating her girls and younger boys at home, Mary was active in acquiring books. She provided reading matter and reading lists to her children as to others, including her daughter-in-law: *Drove to Field's to choose a little library for Lewie to take to sea.* (6/6.7.1863); *Wrote early to Amy sending her a list of books to read.* (15/24.10.1891)

8 By the preoccupations of the age -religion, science, travel etc.

9 By reviews, correspondence and the reactions of others.

10 By the need for religious stimulus and comfort.

Many times Mary recorded that she had been reading, but was unspecific about what she had read; it may be that, in these cases, she was reading newspapers or journals or other material not in book form. On the whole, because of time constraints, it seems unlikely that she could have read many more books than those she named. Rarely, it seemed, did she give up on a text, but there are examples, such as *Tried to read Dean Mansel's Lectures but found them very heavy.* (10/7.3.1875); *Tried to read One of Our Conquerors by George Meredith. The language affected & sentences involved. Professor Drummond mentions George Meredith among authors young men ought to read & this made me send for the book.* (15/28.10.1891)

Biography and autobiography were favourites with Mary, so she read the lives, letters and diaries of many well-known figures, especially when she was already familiar with their written work, including Fanny Kemble, John Keats, Harriet Martineau, Marianne North, Mary Frampton, Susan Huntington, Samuel Pepys, George Crabbe, William Russell, Laurence Oliphant and Queen Victoria.

Clerical subjects included John Jewel, Stopford Brooke, Frederick Farrar, John Stevens Henslow, Richard Cecil, Daniel Wilson, Samuel Wilberforce, James Pycroft, Charles Blomfield, Edward Bickersteth, Thomas Cranmer, John Joseph Gurney, George Selwyn, Norman McCleod, Stopford Brooke, Frederick Robertson, John Tulloch, Augustus Hare, William Harness, John Wesley, Frederick Maurice, Sir Thomas More and Richard Whately.

There were general benefactors, James Goodenough, Elizabeth Fry, John Howard, Sister Dora, Amelia Sieveking.

There were scientists and engineers - Faraday, Stephenson, Newton, Darwin etc. and travellers, explorers and plant-hunters, especially those with Christian motivation. Included in this category were David Livingstone and a number of other explorers of Africa, Robert Fortune (China), Amelia Edwards (Nile), William Ellis (Madagascar), James Tennant (Ceylon), Arthur Evans

(Bosnia), Alexander Hutchinson (Lapland), Johann George Kohl (Russia and Lake Superior), Arthur Young (Ireland) Dorothy Wordsworth (Scotland).

There were also many men and women of letters, such as Charles Dickens, George Eliot, Robert Browning, Charlotte Brontë; public figures and politicians like William Pitt and Lord Palmerston. All these reflect Mary's interest in people and their life histories especially if, like herself, she saw them to be on a spiritual journey.

A substantial proportion of her reading reflected her interest in gardening, botany and natural history. She read Westwood and Humphreys on British butterflies (2/26.8.1852), Hewitson's *Coloured Illustrations of The Eggs of British Birds* (4/4.4.1857); and Newman on *A history of British Ferns* (4/24.12.1857); also some more quirky texts such as Heath, *My Garden Wild*, 1891 (15/8.8.1892) and Lubbock, *Beauties of Nature*, 1893 (16/7.1.1893). Beginning in childhood, Mary read general scientific books, accounts of plant hunters, and much on botany and gardening, but her botanical studies gradually became dominated by major reference works such as Sowerby's *English Botany*. Her reading became more specific according to her progress through the botanical families which she was documenting. For example, **she related that she** (daughter Gracie) **brought me a new Edition of Tripps' British mosses to look at** (13/6.11.1884). However, more entertaining material still occupied her, so that she reported Harding, her gardener, reading **an interesting little book on Natural History by Sir John Lubbock.** (13/21.11.1884). She, herself, a few weeks later, read *a nice little book 'Holiday Excursions of a Naturalist.'* (13/21.11.1884). Nearly a year later, *Familiar Wild Flowers* by F. Edward Hulme, was *cut up* (it contained coloured plates) *& placed in the botanical collection with the corresponding dried specimens.* (14/20.11.1885)

On one occasion, Mary wrote: *Harding came up & I shewed him the figure in Sowerby of the... nympheoides, roots of which he got yesterday out of the Nene.* (13/3. 10.1884). Such sharing of literary information was very common. Towards the end of 1886, Mary referred to the 'Huntly circulating Library' and, soon after, she wrote: *Harding quoted information he has received from the books of travel respecting conifers in their native countries & seems to appreciate the library & to find that others do so.* (14/2.1.1887)

A few weeks later, she *read and looked through European botanical books in the evening* (10/21.1.1887) and, the year after that *copied out a list of interesting plants & their habitats from the old Catalogue of Hunts Flora.* (14/31.1.1888). Also, in 1888, she wrote: *An old Baedecker informs me that the Flora found among the ruins of the Colisseum comprises 420 species which have been collected by an English botanist,* though, she considers, *the number must now be greatly reduced.* (14/15.4.1888). She *wrote to Mr. Drummond thanking him for the loan of the Flora of the Colisseum & asking if he could recommend a book giving the natural history of Rome & its Environs.* (14/26.4.1888). The same year, Mary looked *through a little book purchased at the Library, 'Flowers & Ferns of Cromer.'* (15/10.9.1888) Some years later, during a prolonged illness, her *children read to* (her) *from Miss North's recollections of a Happy life - a delightful book.* (15/9.3.1892)

This autobiographical narrative, detailing notable female accomplishments, was thus shared between the generations.

The aforegoing account of Mary's reading in these later years illustrates the depths of her book research on botanical subjects. Within her reading as with her friends and activities, the local and familiar were nearly always of more interest to Mary than national concerns. In 1883, *Mr. Tylecot the clergyman & his brother came to dinner the former told me that a schoolmaster in the district has published an account of the botany of the neighbourhood.* (13/16.9.1883). She wrote in 1884 to *Mr. Berkeley thanking him for his paper on the natural history of the country round Peterborough, & a medieval brooch dug up at Wood Newton.* (13/27.5.1884). In 1890, she read bits from a book *Rides over England in the 17th Century* by Celia Fiennes commenting: **Her description of Burghley** (the large property neighbouring her childhood home at Uffington) *is very curious.* (15/27.2.1890)

Mary also read books on fine art and architecture and the art of homemaking; also quirky and eccentric books such as Hare's *Walks in London,* Galton's *Hereditary Genius,* Helps' *Friends in Council,* Hawthorne's *Our Old Home,* Trench's *On the Study of Words,* Holmes' *Autocrat of the Breakfast Table*; also social commentary, such as Greville's *Gentlewoman in Society,* Farrar's *Social and Present Day Questions,* Lee's *Divorce or Faithful and Unfaithful,* Mill's *The Subjection of Women.*

Then there were novels. She read a number of these throughout her life, but a larger concentration in the latter stages when she was less capable of dealing with heavier material. Sometimes she approved the stories, using such epithets as 'clever', 'amusing', 'pretty' or 'interesting.' Occasionally she described them as 'stupid' or implied that they were strange. 'Stupid' books seemed often to annoy her more than controversial ones and she spoke of them dismissively.

What effect the books otherwise had upon her is frequently difficult to gage. Whilst much of the religious and biographical reading seems to have sunk deep into her spirit, and historical and informative works added to her knowledge and effectiveness as educator and philanthropist, the more extreme controversies, religious or social, seem, with few exceptions, to have had small effect on her beliefs, actions or preoccupations, though perhaps providing food for her many discussions. Reading appeared, if anything, to consolidate her Christian faith and practice. In this respect she could be compared to the fictional wife of Robert Elsmere who, in the novel of that title, when her clergyman husband turned to religious scepticism, was totally unable to either follow or understand him; the difference is that Mary seems to have read the words of the doubters relatively calmly and with comprehension, while Elsmere's wife, tied to him as she was by the marital bond, found the experience deeply distressing.

Below is a chronological selection of Mary's comments on a variety of works:

I am now reading 'Kenilworth' and am very much interested with it. (16.11.1833) (Age 11)

Reading 'The Buccaneer'.... I liked it very much. (15.4.1834) (Age 11)

I read some of 'Guy Mannering' before I got up this morning and was very much amused with it. (21.4.1834) (Age 11)

I began reading 'Woodstock'. Liked it very much. (13.5.1834) (Age 12)

Wrote the 'Faerie Queen' from a book of Ancient Poetry in the library and I thought it very pretty. (23.6?.1834) (Age 12)

I began reading in bed this morning 'Of Men and Manners in America'... It is I think a clever work. (3.8.1834) (Age 12)

I began reading 'The Fair Maid of Perth' having finished the 'St Ronans Well.' I liked it but thought it ended very bad. (9.8.1834) (Age 12)

I read Blair's Sermon ... it was an exceedingly good sermon. (10.8.1834) (Age 12)

'The Talisman'- very much pleased with it. (22.10.1834) (Age 12)

Reading 'Peveril of the Peak' and am very much amused with it. (11.12.1834) (Age 12)

I began reading 'Contarini Fleming' by D'Israeli (8.1.1835) (Age 12)
(Continued reading) ... It is very wild, but clever. (9.1.1835) (Age 12)

'Quentin Durward' ... very much pleased with it. (31.1.1835) (Age 12)

'Michael Armstrong' by Mrs. Trollope - I was interested by a kind of horrible fascination to her fearful? account of the suffering of the unfortunate factory children. (23.10.1840)

Received Newman's 'British Ferns' from Lady C. Denison. The descriptions are well written by a true lover of Ferns, & the drawings are strikingly accurate. (1/24.12.1847)

Read Passages From 'Life of a Daughter at Home' - much impressed with it. (1/24.3.1848)

'Female Jesuit'- horrid book. (2/27.11.1851)

Miss Brewster's 'Plenty to do & how to do it' - a profitable little book. (3/2.9.1855)

Grindon - He maintains on Scriptural grounds that the soul has a spiritual body, a counterpart of the natural body which exists unseen to mortal eyes after the separation by death from the natural body... Mr. Stephen read aloud to us a chapter from my book on the advantage of the study of Natural History to the young & the charm which a love of it gives to existence. (3/11.11.1856)

'Life of George Stephenson' ... the industry & perseverance of one man. (4/17.11.1857)

'Helen and Olga'- stupid book. (4/6.1.1858)

On the lawn ... interesting conversation on 'Origin of Species'. (5/15.2.1860)

Mary reading aloud 'Dr. Kitto's Life', a wonderful history. (5/17.10.1860)

Read aloud from 'Kohl's Wanderings round Lake Superior' - His accounts of the Indians most interesting. (5/1.12.1860)

The book entitled 'Essays & Reviews' now making a great commotion in the religious world. (5/19.2.1861)

Read sermons entitled 'Science in Theology' (by Adam Farrar) very interesting - one on the economy of pain, another on the atonement. (5/24.3.1861)

2nd vol of 'Les Miserables'; Too harrowing! (6/30.7.1862)

Little book entitled 'Our Babes in Heaven' from Lady Caroline which I liked much reading. (6/31.12.1862)

Began reading Kinglake's 'Invasion of the Crimea' - beautifully written. (6/28.1.1863)

Georgie read aloud a book called 'Artemis Ward.' /American/ which amused us very much. (6/10.2.1863)

Read some of a stupid book by Wilkie Collins called 'No name'. (6/20.2.1863)

Found my fossil heads described in Lyell & compared the originals with the plate. (6/3.3.1863)

Talked over Lyell's 'Antiquity of Man' & Colenso. (6/12.3.1863)

Read 'The Graver thoughts of a Country Parson' & liked it very much. (6/2.8.1863)

Began reading with much interest Stanley's 'Lectures on the Jewish Church.' (6/16.8.1863)

Read 'The Commonplace Philosopher in Town & Country' by Boyd. Some clever & original thoughts. (6/9.5.1864)

Read a little pamphlet by Dr Brown called 'Marjorie Fleming'- a true account of a precocious little girl & very affecting. (7/27.7.1864)

Read 'Robertson's Life and Letters' showing the struggles to see truth of an earnest & devout mind. (7/19.11.1865)

Read Newman's 'Apologia' - showing I think how Romish principles, though unsuspected by their possessor, end in Rome. (7/11.3.1866)

Baker's 'Albert N'yanza Great Basin of the Nile' very amusing and well written. (7/11.8.1866)

Read Goulbourn's 'Personal Religion' & propose reading a chapter every day. (7/12.8.1866)

Read 'Lady Audley's Secret' as a specimen of a sensational novel. (7/11.9.1866)

'Clarissa' ... clever as Richardson may be he shows no taste for romances. (8/20.10.1868)

Read 'The Gay Science' 1866 by Mr. Dallas (Mary knew him personally) with so much interest. (Gay science is by Nietzche, first published in 1882). (8/26.10.1868)

Read Tennyson's new book of poems 'The Holy Grail'... very inferior it strikes me to what he has written before. (8/28.1.1870)

Read Browning's 'Paracelsus' which I thought very forcible & affecting. (9/27.8.1871)

Found a curious book 'The Fables of John Dryden' ornamented with engravings from the pencil of the Right Honourable - Lady Diana

Beauclerc - she of whom we have the picture at Orton- published 1797. (9/11.1.1872)

Read 'Erewhon' (Nowhere) a curious book. (9/11.11.1872)

Charlotte read 'Simple Susan' to the children- & I listened with as much pleasure as they. (9/9.12.1872)

Finished reading 'The Eustace Diamonds' by Trollope. The character of Lizzie Eustace clear but very disagreeable. (9/15.1.1873)

Sir Charles showed me the unique edition of the 'Venus & Adonis of Shakespeare' said to be worth £1000 (9/6.2.1873)

And 'Lord Pembroke's Roots' - a curious book (book not traced). (9/8.9.1873)

Read 'Lorna Doone' by R.D. Blackmore which gave a good description of the scenery in these parts. (10/26.9.1874)

Began to read Dorothy Wordsworth's tour of Scotland with William ... showing marvellous change in the country during 70 years. (10/27.2.1875)

Read J.S. Mill's '3 Essays on Religion.' There is something animating & suggestive in the thought at the end that human beings have it in their power to cooperate with a Superior & Beneficent being for good in the present, & for the ultimate triumph of good in the future. (10/28.2.1875)

Read 'Social Pressure' by Sir Arthur Helps who has lately died to the great regret of the Queen. (10/11.3.1875)

Read 2 volumes of a stupid novel called 'Queenie'. (10/31.5.1875)

Read 'Mr Smith- A Part of His Life' by L B Walford- a most amusing well-written story. (10/28.10.1875)

Read 'Elia', the charming essays by Lamb. (10/29.11.1875)

Read Livingstone's 'Last Journals' and they are very affecting. In the midst of cruelty and degradation he yet could look forward to the regeneration *of Africa though aware that he should never see it in the flesh.* (10/6.12.1875)

'A Memoir of Commodore Goodenough' by Markham - a really good and great man. (10/13.2.1876)

Finished Macaulay biography - a wonderfully happy life & painless death. His reading was a perpetual feast of soul to him. (10/3.9.1876, begun 10/14.7.1876)

Read Thomas Hope's 'Anastasius' a picture of Turkish manners a 100 years ago which might have been drawn today. (10/27.10.1876)

Read a little book bought at the station yesterday called 'A Plea for Art' in the House which am going to send to Nellie. (10/28.11.1876)

Children read aloud from 'Smiles' Life of a Scotch Naturalist' which much amused them. (10/11.12.1876) (Continued reading)- *All full of 'Life of a Scotch Naturalist'.* (10/14.12.1876)

Looked through an interesting book entitled 'Illustrations of Cheshire' (book not traced).

Wished I could do something of the same kind for Hunts. (11/18.9.1878)

Went out & spoke to Harding about rose culture being inspired by Canon Hole's book about roses. (11/5.12.1878)

Read 'Robert Dick Geologist and Botanist' by Smiles an interesting biography of a Scotch baker. There is mention of his friend Peach of Wansford son of a saddle and harness maker there. (11/30.12.1878)

Read on the way a horrid & sensational novel, 'The Haunted Hotel' by Wilkie Collins. (11/7.11.1879)

Read Miss Burney's 'Evelina'. Certainly manners have improved after the lapse of 100 years. (11/8.11.1879)

Read 'Our Village' by Miss Mitford and an extract from Henry Mackenzie's Man of Feeling- an evident imitation of Sterne. (12/23.2.1880)

Finished 3rd volume of McCarthy - very pleasant reading. (12/9.11.1880)

Read George Eliot's 'Scenes from Clerical life' - that entitled Rev Amos Barton very affecting. (12/19.2.1881)

Read 'The Autocrat of the Breakfast Table' by an American, Holmes containing many nice thoughts. (13/23.9.1883)

Read the last part of Wilberforce's 'Life'. The end was touching. (13/28.10.1883)

Read 'Altiora Peto' by Laurence Oliphant - very clever. (13/27.11.1883)

Finished 'Dr Claudius' - very clever. (13/26.1.1884)

'Tale of Two Cities' - rather a creepy book. I had not read it before. (13/13.5.1884)

Finished the 'Life of Princess Alice' - very touching in its self abnegation & devotion to the good of others. (13/29.6.1884)

Maurice of high interest. (13/5.8.1884)

Read some interesting sermons preached in England by an American Philip Brooks - Not sure *if this is the version - preached in England?* (13/31.8.1884)

Wrote to Marsh sending him the 4th part of Colenso's book on the Pentateuch which he wished to see. (13/12.9.1884)

Read a stupid book called 'Eyre's Acquittal'. (13/25.11.1884)

Read 'Lectures on the Industrial Revolution' by the late Arnold Toynbee ... are very interesting but I was not able to give them as much attention as they deserve. (13/4.1.1885)

Read 'An American Politician' by Marion Crawford which is interesting as an explanation of yankee statesmanship. (13/12.1.1885)

Read an interesting book with rather a foolish title 'The Sagacity and Morality of Plants' by J E Taylor containing a good deal of true science. (13/3.4.1885)

Read a novel 'Rogues and Vagabonds' or some such name considered good. (13/25.7.1885)

Began reading 'Autobiography of Christopher

Kirkland' by Lynn Linton beginning with a description of the people and laws of England 60 years ago & reminding one of the gradual changes which have brought about a better state of things each of which changes has been pronounced Radical and dangerous & therefore resisted in its turn. (14/13.3.1886)

Read the 'Rise of Silas Lapham' by Howells an American. Rather clever. (14/9.7.1886)

Read a curious story by Mrs Praed called 'Nadine' founded upon facts which have occurred in real life. (14/16.12.1886)

Read curious book, 'The New Republic' by W H Mallock. (14/28.12.1886)

Read a book of Granville's - She by Haggard the author of 'King Solomon's Mines' but I did not like it as I do not care for books treating of impossible occurrences told with all the audacity of simple truth. (14/29.1.1887)

Read 'Moths' by Ouida 1880 recommended by Amy. Clever but a painful story. (14/29.9.1887)

Read 'The Light of Asia' by Edward Arnold-beautifully written. (14/20.10.1887)

Finished McCarthy's book - very clever. (14/13.11.1887)

Read 'Mona's Choice' by Mrs Alexander- a pretty story but not well written. (14/3.12.1887)

Worked and read 'The Professor' by Currer Bell one of her first works and very clever. (14/17.3.1888)

Read the much-talked of 'Robert Elsmere' by Mrs Humphrey Ward which was reviewed in the Spring by Gladstone. (15/3.12.1888)

Finished a book entitled 'Faithful & unfaithful' turning upon the laws of divorce in the United States & reviewed by Mr Gladstone. The character of the faithful wife very fine. (15/3.6.1889)

Read a Curious Book – 'The Autobiography of Mark Rutherford' by Reuben Shapcott. (15/5.9.1889)

Read Stanley's 'Life of Dr Arnold' renewing my recollections of it 40 years ago. (15/11.12.1889)

Read 'Frederick the Noble' by Sir Morrell Mackenzie giving his description of the poor Emperor's terrible illness & his quarrels with the German doctors The sale of this book has since been prohibited. (15/16.2.1890)

To Mr Sharpe thanking him for his opinion of Mr Hake's book. (15/2.5.1890)

Charlotte read aloud from rather a stupid book, 'The Search for Basil Lyndhurst'. (15/17.2.1891)

Read 'Paul Nugent-Materialist' a kind of answer to Robert Elsmere. (15/9.3.1891)

Read a rather interesting story 'Basil & Annette'. (15/10.4.1891)

One of Canon Farrar's sermons out of a little book given me by Mary on my birthday. (15/3.5.1891)

Miss P read aloud from 'A Sensitive Plant' by E D Gerrard while I embroidered. (Mary discussed qualities in the characters). (15/22.7.1891)

Worked & read life of Laurence Oliphant. His is

an extraordinary character. A wonderful faith & earnestness in acting up to his convictions perplexing as these were at times. Primitive Christianity however was always his model. (15/29.8.1891)

Finished the book on the 'Development of Africa' by A Silva White - principally statistical but interesting. (15/11.10.1891)

Began reading 'History of Hampton Court Palace in Orange & Guelph times' by Earnest Law. Interesting & well illustrated but the author's interests are all Jacobite. (15/26.10.1891)

Received from Wilson, 'Moggridge's Flora' - beautifully illustrated & as good as new. (15/30.10.1891)

Charlotte read aloud from a book of Mrs Needell's – 'Unequally Yoked' which is fairly good. (15/23.11.1891)

Mrs Sibthorp(?) of Lincoln Sends me a little book containing her drawings of flowers in Norway & wishing me to help her with some of the names. (15/8.12.1891)

Charlotte read to me aloud from 'Darkness &

Dawn' - an account of the Times of Nero by Archdeacon Farrar- very interesting. (15/13.12.1891)

Read Carlyle's 'Past and Present' - to me most interesting. (15/20.12.1891)

Read 'The Gentlewoman in Society' by Mrs Greville - clever & amusing. (15/26.12.1891)

Read 'Lady Faint Heart' illustrating the change in a girl's heart from philosophical to religious views. (15/3.6.1891)

I read 'Essays in the History of Religious Thought in the West' by D Westcott of Durham - a very interesting book. (15/31.12.1891)

Read an amusing book, 'The Penance of Portia James' by Tasma. Charlotte read to me from King Squash of Toadyland written by a foreign diplomat who has lived in this country but name not given. It is a keen criticism of English society & politics & clever. (15/27.2.1892)

Worked & began reading the popular novel, 'The History of David Grieve' by Mrs Humphrey Ward (financial details given by Mary of what money she made). (15/2.4.1892)

Finished 'The Railway Man' - an amusing book only those who behave the worst seem to get off best in the end. (15/21.4.1892)

Read with much interest one of the Modern Science series 'The Cause of an Ice Age' by Robert S Ball edited by Sir John Lubbock. The cause is attributed to the disturbances of the Earth's path by the influence of Jupiter & Venus - & as several Ice Ages have already occurred in the history of the Earth so may they occur again. (15/18.6.1892)

Clark sends some notes upon 'The Douglas Book' by William Fraser. (16/17.11.1892)

Ethel read aloud from a charming book by Sir John Lubbock, 'The Beauties of Nature', while I worked. (16/7.1.1893)

Worked & looked through some of that delightful book, 'Green's History of the English People', lent me by Fanny. (16/21.2.1893)

Looked at a new illustrated edition of Green's 'History of the English People' now coming out. (16/15.3.1893)

> Miss P read aloud to me from 'The Heavenly Twins' – an extraordinary book. (16/5.6.1893)

> Reading Canon Westcott's 'Gospel of Life' - a very interesting book. (16/28.6.1893)

> Gracie sent me a book called 'A Mere Cypher' by Mary A Dickens. It is very exciting & absorbing. (16/1.7.1893)

Finally, in this chapter, it is fascinating to note how Mary integrated life and literature. This began in childhood when, for example, she was especially prone to quote Southey. She declared one night:

> *I felt ready to exclaim with Southey "How beautiful is night!" ... Who is there also while looking upon the Queen of Light who does not remember the many who may at that moment be thinking the same thoughts & praying the same thoughts with yourself.* (22.9.1839)

Again, describing a storm, Mary wrote *Southey's touching lines crossed my mind & I thought "upon the suffering mariners."* (24.1.1840). Similarly, in her latter years, she wrote *Beautiful Night, not a leaf moving, reminding me of Southey's lines in Thalaba.* (13/29.6.1883). It was recounted earlier how Mary listened, as a child, to Charlotte reciting this poem; clearly this had impressed itself deeply upon her memory.

In 1843, meeting some gypsies, Mary was reminded of Wordsworth's 'We are Seven' since they shared *the conviction and the pain of a separation between the dead & the living* (7.3.1843). Then, a touching example occurred when she *read Dr. Kitto on 'wearisome nights'* and exclaimed *How often I have realized his description* (6/13.2.1862). After Strath's death, Mary read Tennyson's 'In Memoriam', clearly trying to take comfort from the sentiments expressed (6/13.12.1863). More prosaically, she ***Gave H the Life of John Duncan Weaver & Botanist to read & this led to our talking over the rarer Aberdeenshire plants.*** (15/28.1.1889)

However, the deepest link between literature and life occurred in Mary's application of the Scriptures and the contents of sermons to her daily life. She recounted them continually and committed them to her memory. A most sad example refers to a late, much beloved son.

Read a sermon of Robertson in which he speaks of the true character as a reflection of the Divine and this may be applied to dear Douglas. (15/12.8.1888)

3

The Books: Consolidating Faith

Is it not strange, that the only persons who appear to me to carry to the grave with them the joyousness, simplicity, and lovingness and trust of children, are the most exalted Christians?
(Charles Kingsley: His Letters and Memories of His Life, 1877)
vol 1, p.106. (11/1.4.1877)

Oh that one felt sure that as one irresistibly travels onward that one advanced spiritually.
Mary's Diaries (1/1.1.1848)

Whilst, at this time of religious questioning, there were many from whom faith departed, there were also many who devotedly continued to pursue their Christian religion. Mary was very much one of the latter. Clearly, according with the culture of her childhood and her own Christian passion, she was not only a believer, but of the opinion that Christianity was a great blessing and a powerful force for civilisation. She read widely within religious literature, encountering both the texts which reinforced her own outlook and afforded her comfort and those more controversial ones which called her views into question or blatantly contradicted them. This chapter looks primarily at the first, the next chapter at the second.

Mary lived her life surrounded by Christian clergy, both as relatives and friends, including her father, Rev Peter Pegus; friends, Rev. Charles Kingsley, novelist and Church of England Priest, Rev. Miles Joseph Berkeley, Rev. Charles Wolley-Dod and other so-called 'botanical clergy.' From early years, she was imbued with the religious practices of daily prayer, family worship, reading of Scripture, sermons and tracts and Sunday observance. She lived her religion, practised philanthropy, and carefully instructed her children and her servants in the Scriptures. She admired those she perceived to be good and heroic, highly approving such men as Dr David Livingstone, physician, celebrated African explorer and Christian missionary; Commander James Goodenough, naval officer and devoted Christian; and John Howard, exemplary Christian leader, philanthropist and early

English prison reformer; and she read their biographies along with many others.

She pondered on spiritual dilemmas, such as *the difficulty of hating the sin without being angry with the sinners* (2/18.11.1852) and engaged in theological discussions (see below), but seemingly never wavered in her belief or her Christian observances. The solemn and regular repetition in her diary of her pious thoughts and practices could engender boredom or irritation in those looking for narrative excitement, but ultimately her gentle, yet tenacious, spirit wins admiration. Undoubtedly, Mary often sought comfort and religious confirmation and, in her adult years, she read the works of some favoured preachers repeatedly- Stopford Brooke, Charles Kingsley, Charles Vaughan and others, but her favourite was certainly Frederick Robertson, of whose sermons she seems to have had a copy perpetually to hand, increasingly as the years progressed. Entries like the following are frequent: *Read Robertson & a nice little book entitled The Practice of the Presence of God by Brother Lawrence sent me by Mrs Jane Dundas.* (8/24.11.1867); *Read the service & Robertson* 15/22.9.1889); *Read service & Robertson.* (15/19.7.1891)

She enjoyed sermons characterised by love, humanity, devotion to God, and practical advice for everyday life, but also those with themes of suffering and chastisement (deemed to be heaven-sent), noting the topics of the sermons read weekly in the estate church with their appropriate gospel readings. Throughout life, but increasingly in the few years prior to her death, she referred to her Christian religion in terms of spiritual and emotional support. In 1891, when she was too weak to attend church, she described the sacrament administered to herself and Ethel at home as *comforting as have not been able to go to church for so long.* (15/21.8.1891). In 1892, she commented on the books that arrived from Day and Son:

> Began reading *There is No Death by Florence Marryat (&) Rambles of a Dominie, the first author a spiritualist, the latter a naturalist, the latter to my mind the more soothing of the two.* (15/22.1.1892)

The naturalist, focusing on the works of God, appealed to her spirit more than the non-Christian spiritualist. In 1893, close to her death, she **continued Charles Kingsley's Life which is quite delightful & very soothing to me.** (16/4.6.1893)

The benefits of Christianity on a national or worldwide basis were extolled at this time and often framed as a gift of European nations to other countries:

> "It is undoubtedly true that under ordinary circumstances Christianity precedes rather than succeeds civilisation. Religion begins from within and works outwards, first making the heart right, and then afterwards the life." (Farrar, Science in Theology, 1859) p.98. fn. (5/24.3.1861)

> "The essential connection of Christianity with the history of past ages makes a provision for the maintenance and advancement of civilization in every country in which

Christianity prevails." (Thompson, *Aids to Faith*, 1861) p.65. (6/27.7.1862)

"This it was which tamed the wild flood of northern barbarians into the Christendom of Europe. This it was which made childhood sacred, and ennobled womanhood, and turned poverty into a beatitude. This it was which founded the greatness of England, and led the Pilgrim Fathers to America," (Farrar, *Social and Present Day Questions*, 1892) p.138. (15/22.5.1892)

Some put forward a different view:

"The crude truth is, that nine-tenths of foreign missions are not got up for the benefit of the heathen abroad, but for the good of the sect at home." (Herbert, *South Sea Bubbles*, 1872) p.299. (9/2.7.1872)

Mary again heartily endorsed the positive view: **Read History of the Roman Emperors by Lynam. It makes me realize the benefits which Christianity has bestowed upon the world.** (12/31.1.1882). She recognised that cruelty was not confined to older civilisations: **Read a biography of Howard the Philanthropist. What barbarities existed in civilized countries- 100 years ago & later.** (13/28.12.1884)

She shared, with many of her coevals, a preoccupation with sects, denominations and high and low church, although not identifying herself too closely with any: **Told us that many of the scientific men in London were Swedenborgians; we looked out**

& read the articles of their faith in the Penny Cyclopedia. (2/ 30.12.1853); *Papa's impression of my 'Calvinism.'* (3/29.1.1854); *She* (Miss Ladame) *told me she had fears that Miss Hildegard is a Tractarian if not a Roman Catholic.* (4/27.4.1857); *Had some talk with him* (Mr Mackenzie) *about the tenets of the Plymouth Brethren. He lent us a book by Miss Whately on the subject.* (14/24.8.1885); *Marsh arrived. He told me much about Lord Sebright's preaching & the work of the Salvation Army at Fakenham which he much approves.* (15/1.7.1889); *He* (McKay) *told me of the division of religious opinions in the Free Church.* (15/10.4.1890); *Finished reading Broad Church. What he* (Haweis) *says of Mesmerism, Spiritualism & Hypnotism is curious and interesting.* (15/15.6.1891); *Finished reading A Short Life of John Wesley.* (15/27.7.1891); *Read an account of the Anabaptists of Munster by Baring Gould.* (15/2.3.1892)

Also:

> *Read England & Rome A History of Relations between the Papacy & the English State ... It proves clearly that Q Elizabeth & the English nation were driven to enact penal laws against the Papists not from any intolerance towards the Roman Catholic religion but as a necessary protection from State dangers & intrigues.* (15/14.8.1892)

Mary eagerly read the works of those of diverse denominations, caring more for the essence of religion than its forms and divisions, as mirrored in the views of a number of clergy, including Robertson, her favourite preacher:

"*More than half the heresies into which Christian sects have blundered, have merely come from mistaking for dull prose what prophets and apostles said in those highest moments of the soul, when seraphim kindle the sentences of the pen and lip into poetry.*" (Robertson, *Sermons*, 2nd Series, 1855-19 *The Good Shepherd*) (Robertson, *Sermons Preached at Brighton, by the late Rev. Frederick W. Robertson*, New York: Harper, 1905) p.407. (1860 onwards)

Mary's father, Peter Pegus, was a clergyman of the Church of England; whilst espousing some evangelical views and practices, Mary was not bound by them and, though she read some purely evangelical texts from such as Bishop J.C. Ryle, the great tract writer, in her early days, later some of her favourite writers were those who had outgrown pure evangelicalism such as Stopford Brooke and Frederick Robertson, as well as straight Church of England clerics or Broad Church writers like Thomas Arnold, Charles Kingsley and Arthur Penhryn Stanley; she also read High Church and Tractarian writers like John Henry Newman.

There was, in fact, something of a backlash against evangelicalism:

"*This is what the evangelicals do in another way. They make two Gods, a loving one and an angry one, - the former saving from the latter.*" (Robertson; Brooke, *Life and Letters of F.W. Robertson*, 1865) vol 2, p.56. (7/19.11.1865)

"*But as regarded what was called Evangelical Religion or*

Puritanism, there was more to cause alarm; but on the other hand it had no intellectual basis; no internal idea, no principle of unity, no theology." (Newman, *Apologia Pro Vita Sua*, 1865) p.200. (Oxford University Press, 1913). (7/11.3.1866)

"The exclusive spirit of the Evangelicals (so called) and their common mode of speaking of others have always been repugnant to me." (Hare, A., *Memorials of a Quiet Life*, 1873) p.159. (1872). (9/21.8.1873)

Mary made little comment on this. Even within her 'approved' group, the preachers and religious writers were divergent in their styles and theological viewpoints. J.C. Ryle, for example, heavily reliant on warnings of hellfire, declaring that few would be saved, whilst Farrar propounded the opposite view of God's mercifulness to all and the incompatibility of the more graphic depictions of physical hell with God's nature. Mary did not record any reading of Farrar's *Eternal Hope*, where his view is most clearly expressed, and made no comment on this disparity; she may, indeed, not have encountered the relevant expressions of opinion or understood or analysed them in these terms, but the lack of comment, at least in her diary, on some of the deepest religious controversies, is remarkable. She seemed open to a wide range of interpretations of Christian doctrine, at least in understanding, if not in practice.

She took stock of her progress in life, mainly in terms of spiritual advancement. Far from her worldly concerns, she engaged in an amount of self-talking aimed at her improvement and readiness for the world to come and, following a tradition of diary writers on a similar spiritual journey, she tended to make assessments on birthdays and at the transition between one year and the next:

> *The Lord loveth whom he chasteneth... Oh, how I pray my Almighty Father in His great mercy to help me to become better by this time next year that another 12 months of this short life may not have passed so unworthily as the preceding ones (thanks for former blessings ... & what a watch I ought to keep over myself!* (This is Mary's brave entry at the end of the year in which her sister Elizabeth died.) (31.12.1837)

Also:

> *Feeling my spiritual deadness I am anxious at the beginning of another year to keep some record of my state.* (2/2.1.1853)

> *Seeing very much to deplore in myself in the last year.* (3/31.12.1854)

> *If spared during this may it be one of spiritual improvement.* (15/1.1.1892)

Books provided Mary with an extension of her own religious world, for religious texts were not only abundant in the literature of the century but also predominant in her own reading:

> "*Souls are being quickened and edified by the instrumentality of books, which books are all that remain of their authors.*" (Goulbourn, *Thoughts on Personal Religion*, 1864) p.107. (7/12.8.1866)

She read many books of sermons from childhood onwards. As usual, she also read what was current in educated circles and the preoccupation with religion permeated every genre. This included novels which tended either to contain passages of religious and philosophical speculation or to be almost entirely based on such. One prominent example is Mrs Humphrey Ward's *Robert Elsmere*, which describes the devastating consequences of the loss of belief on a fictional clergyman and the even more disastrous effect on his wife, a devoted believer, not entirely unlike Mary in her unwavering faith; other examples are *The Autobiography of Mark Rutherford* and Margaret Deland's *John Ward Preacher*.

Religious and philosophical discussions were prevalent in the circles in which Mary moved and took place between friends, relatives, clergy and educated members of the laity, sometimes on points of minor theological difference, sometimes on more profound or divisive issues. Mary was also only too happy to engage in these, though we are often not provided with the details of them or the prevailing tone of the conversations.

The following is a sample, from the diary, of references to such conversations:

Had much interesting conversation with Boden on religious subjects. (1/6.12.1848); *Long talk with H.L. about deep matters connected with religion the moral sense & original sin.* (1/21.1.1849); *He (Mr. Bowen) accompanied us to the shrubbery & afterwards I had a long talk with him in the cloister on spiritual & secular anxieties.* (2/28.1.1853); *Conversation with Papa respecting the consistency of geology & the book entitled 'Essays & Reviews' now making a great commotion in the religious world.* (5/19.2.1861); *Talked over Lyell's Antiquity of man & Colenso.* (6/12.3.1863); *Discussed the theological questions of the day after breakfast.* (6/7.8.1863); *My Aunts eloquent upon the world having only existed about 6000-7000 years- & horrified at my doubts on the subject which approaches in their eyes to infidel opinions.* (6/16.12.1863); *Had a conversation with Hurry upon theology & science.* (7/24.7.1864); *Reading Vaughan and talking on religious subjects with Quintin Hogg.* (7/23.7.1865); *Talking over the deep theological subjects of the day.* (7/24.1.1866); *Theological discussions with Mr. Davies. He considers that salvation only comes through baptism & the Lord's Supper as the appointed channels.* (7/6.4.1866); *Talked with Mr Clark about theology and the tendencies of the religious convictions of the day.* (7/11.10.1866); *Talking over the religious opinions & books of the day.* (8/14.2.1867); *Sat out under the lime trees talking to Sir de Wells(?) about the great theological questions of the day.* (8/29.8.1867); *An interesting conversation with Mr. Smith on theological subjects suggested by one of Froude's Essays.* (8/22.12.1867); *Walked with Mr Dallas and had a long & interesting conversation with him upon theological subjects & the struggles of the soul after truth.* (8/8.11.1868); *Theological talk with Marsh in the evening.* (13/25.8.1882); *Talked over books and the Oxford Movement in the evening with Ethel.* (13/4.4.1883); *Marsh & Charlotte had a long argument for/against the Salvation Army.* (15/6.7.1889)

There are a number of doctrines which Mary encountered both in her religious life and in her reading, to which she paid due reverence, and her commitment was often reinforced through the effect of the recent evangelical revival on English Society. The first topic, **social divisions**, discussed here, is related less to doctrine than to an understanding/presumption that pervaded many social and Christian texts. We move then to a primary teaching of Christianity, that of **unworldliness,** followed by the **focus on home, family and separate spheres,** which was broadly influential in Victorian Society. Allied to this is the **elevation of ordinary life** as a main sphere of operation and of Christian worship, and then the notion of **duty.** Next **faith versus works** and **heart versus intellect** are discussed and, associated with these, the necessity of **approaching religion as a child. Scripture** is a discrete topic; **Heaven and Hell** follow, and then the two faces of divine intervention, **providence and chastening.**

Inherited from past centuries came the view that **social divisions** were ordained by God and to be accepted submissively. Loyalty to family and the traditions of her upbringing ensured that Mary, like others of her class, upheld the customs of aristocracy, though the Liberal political world in which she moved, alongside the Christian doctrines to which she adhered and her own tender-mindedness, often generated conflict within her, and she may have been additionally influenced by the developing socialism of her oldest son who wrote,

> "Following these lines up on safe grounds, what a future there is for State Socialism! It is the safest and only practicable means of bestowing equal benefits on all classes of our race."

Mary's views on this were mixed and sometimes confused. The mood of her insider commentary on the social and political scene of the landed aristocracy, and of royalty, alternated between boredom and contempt, and she provides a less than flattering picture of many in the upper classes. As a child, describing, in 1837, the local elite attending the horticultural show at Stamford, she described *a great collection of beautiful fruit & ugly people* (21.7.1837). Referring much later to Benjamin Disraeli, she commented, **He ruled in consequence of the inferiority of intellect among the higher classes in England.** (15/25.5.1891). She tended to speak affectionately, though with condescension, of the lower classes. **A pleasant feeling of harmony seemed to permeate all classes.** (3/29.5.1856); *Tropical Gardens, Battersea Park- good to see so many of the lower orders enjoying quiet Sunday.* (12/24.7.1881); **The Spiritual and mental improvement of the menial classes.** (13/17.4.1884). Although Mary's instincts, on an individual basis, were compassionate and egalitarian she talked in this way of the 'lower orders' and had no realistic conception of life outside her own sphere. In terms of socialism, Mary, despite their friendship, described

Charles Kingsley's *Yeast* as a **wild and dangerous book**. However, she disliked exercising authority over social 'inferiors.' It was this very fact that probably most drew the disrespect of underlings, and was a lifelong problem for her as described in Chapter 1.

Thus, whilst enjoying many of its privileges, she took little pleasure in her worldly status, but agreed with the consensus of the age that social position was divinely ordained. Indeed, she prayed for the grace to **do my duty in the station of life to which thou hast been pleased to call me.** (14.10.1840). The demands of her relatives in childhood and of her husband in adulthood necessitated her having to take hierarchy seriously, according to sentiments echoed repeatedly in the social and family life she led and the books she read:

> "*She felt, as all must do, who reflect on the subject, that if all distinctions were by some accident suddenly removed, and the entire organisation of society to begin de novo, each man standing on the same levels as his neighbour, the earth would not complete revolution round the sun, ere the equality would be violated.*" (Trollope, *The Life and Adventures of Michael Armstrong*, 1840) p.97. (23.10.1840)

> "*And this is the extent of the obedience here required, that it be paid to all kinds of masters, not to the good only, but also to the evil; not only to obey, but to suffer, and suffer patiently, and not only deserved, but even wrongful and unjust punishment.*" (Leighton, *A Practical Commentary upon the First*

Epistle of St. Peter, 1845) vol 1, p.386. (Bohn, 1849). (1/30.8.1846)

"In retaining ourselves and regarding in others the simple standing that God has given, there is a native dignity, a moral elevation." (Charlesworth, *Ministering Children*, 1854) p.27. (New York: Riker, 1855). (3/4.9.1855)

"And here I say of clerical meetings and open expressions of social rights, not that they do no good, but that for the last twenty years I have seen them do no little harm." (Pycroft, *Twenty Years in the Church*, 1860) p.232. (1859). (5/16.11.1860)

"I am so far opposed to the levelling principles of the democrats, that I consider it a decided mistake, in persons of higher rank, to try to put those of the lower class exactly on the same footing with themselves. It does them no good, and will probably embarrass them, or make them presuming." (Poel, *Life of Amelia Wilhelmina Sieveking*, 1863) p.443. (6/2.1.1864)

"It seems to me a great mistake to lead the working-classes to suppose that by any means independent of their own energy, moral improvement, and self-restraint, their condition can be permanently altered." (Robertson; Brooke, *Life and letters of Frederick W. Robertson*, 1865) vol 2, p.7. (7/19.11.1865)

"Even the slave's duties may be sanctified by importing into them a Christian motive" (Goulburn, *Thoughts on Personal Religion*, 1864) pp.41-42. (7/12.8.1866)

"He loved to recall the times when servants and masters lived together as members of the same family, with mutual respect and common interests." (L'estrange, *The Literary Life of the Rev. W. Harness*, 1871) p.122. (9/11.3.1872)

"A bad spirit seems to be everywhere at work, and the ties and bonds of society to be loosening amongst all classes. An impatience of restraint and disregard of authorities and government is growing up, and the ignorant alike with the informed cast from them the wholesome ties which formerly restrained them." (Hare, A. *Memorials of a Quiet Life*, 1873) p.361. (1872). (9/21.8.1873)

"God has ordained differences of rank, and intended his Church to pervade all ranks." (Ashwell, *Life of the Right Reverend Samuel Wilberforce*, 1883) p.83. (New York: Dutton). (13/12.10.1883)

"We do not understand the operations of Almighty wisdom, and are therefore unable to tell the causes of the terrible inequalities that we see." (Trollope, *An Autobiography*, 1883) vol 2, p.129. (13/25.2.1884)

"All our existing institutions are those under which God has placed us, under which we are to mould our lives according to His Will." (Robertson, *Sermons on St. Paul's Epistles to the Corinthians*, 1860) p.105. (14/2.1.1887)

There are a number of recurrent themes both in Mary's reading and her comments. One main preoccupation was the requirement for 'unworldliness' and, typically, Mary recorded an *interesting conversation with Lady Exeter upon living in the world and yet not being of the world* (2/23.11.1853), and in later years mentioned a *Letter from Lady Lindsey condemning worldliness* (15/29.10.1891). There would have been some compatibility, but also some tension, between her worldly status and duties to husband, children and servants and a religion which demanded her humility, self-chastening and inattention to worldly things, although it appears that, in his lifetime, Strath, a fellow Christian devotee, gave Christian support.

It is sometimes difficult to distinguish between the manifestations of her own natural inclinations and the dictates of her religion, for example, in her hatred of balls, visiting and other upper middle-class amusements which, in childhood, she shared with Charlotte. The superficials did not interest her and the worldly things which many found exciting, left her cold. The simple, natural things in life made her radiant. She performed many of her social and worldly duties to a minimal degree, and with reluctance, and openly expressed her disgust at fashionable society: *Talked about fashionable society as it is in London which H.L. & I agreed in condemning. Will another generation improve upon it?* (2/20.11.1851). Whilst not shunning the theatre or the playing of cards, at least in her own home, she fell in gladly with the evangelical proscription of worldly pursuits, though attending to them dutifully where required by parents, husband or adolescent children, especially daughters looking to make matches.

Her Christian reading confirmed her in this:

> "It is the ignorance, or at least the inconsideration of Divine things, that makes earthly things, whether good or evil, appear great in our eyes." (Leighton, *Practical Commentary upon the First Epistle of St. Peter*, 1845) p.103. (Bohn, 1849). (1/30.8.1846)

> "They who use the world ought not to use it to the uttermost; ought not to use it with too much of eagerness, too much of absorption in it, too much of addiction to it." (Vaughan, *Lessons of life and Godliness*, 1862) p.315. (6/9.11.1862)

> "All insatiable longing after earthly things, all grasping and restless striving, is a part of that covetousness which is idolatry." (Hare, A., *The Alton Sermons*, 1878) p.497. (1874). (11/1.12.1878)

> "A worldly spirit more repugnant to the love of God and feelings of religion than the state of a real sinner!" (Stanley, *Memoirs of Edward and Catherine Stanley*, 1880) p.147. (2/27.2.1880)

> "Mourn not over what will so soon be irreparably gone.

> There is nothing worth it." (Robertson, Sermons on St. Paul's Epistles to the Corinthians, 1868) p.113. (1860). (14/2.1.1887)

> "And she belonged to that extensive class who would be shocked to hear themselves called irreligious, and yet never let religion stand in the way of comfort, self-indulgence, or worldly success." (Hetherington, Paul Nugent-Materialist, 1891) p.180. (15/9.3.1891)

> "We know the greed and worldliness of society, and the base motives which often predominate in marriage." (Farrar, Social and Present Day Questions, 1892) p.173. (15/22.5.1892)

One of the incentives to unworldliness was the realisation that worldly happiness was an illusion, a perception to which the originally happy spirit of Mary would bow as she progressed through her life:

> "God's promises never are fulfilled in the sense in which they seem to have been given. Life is a deception; ... wise and merciful arrangement which ordains it thus." (Robertson, Sermons, 3rd Series, 1857 - 6 The Illusiveness of Life (Robertson, Sermons Preached at Brighton, by the late Rev. Frederick W. Robertson, New York: Harper, 1905) p.487. (1860 onwards)

Mary's affections and energies were rooted in **home** and **family** but her class position meant that **separate spheres** (for men and women) was, for her, only partially operative. There was no regular separation in the working day between herself and Strath, though they played complementary roles in the running of their estate, with Strath clearly in command. By choice, Mary absented herself from the hunting field and generally cultivated the floral areas of the grounds while Strath spent time on his collection of conifers and his hunting, although they created the main avenue, called The Long Walk, together. According to a traditional female role, she concerned herself with the comfort of the home and direction of the domestic servants and made herself responsible for the upbringing and education, especially the religious education, of the children and the servants, and the wellbeing and good practices of the whole family. Note from her diary, **Family prayers for the first time (very happy about this 'social worship')** (1/21.10.1844); **Huntly read a sermon of Kingsley to the servants.** (1/5.11.1864)

Gendered roles were supported both in evangelical teaching and, increasingly, the general culture. These are examples from Mary's reading:

> "His wife should be above all things, a woman of faith and prayer- a woman too, of a sound mind and of a tender heart- and one who will account it her glory to lay herself out in co-operating with her husband by meeting his wants and soothing his cares." (Cecil, *The life and Remains of the Rev. Richard Cecil*, 1854) p.234. (London: Printed for Seeley, 1816). (3/ 28.9.1856)

> "The glory of true womanhood consists in being herself:

not in striving to be something else. It is the false paradox and heresy of this present age to claim for her as a glory the right to leave her sphere. ... There is one glory of manhood, and another glory of womanhood. And the glory of each created thing consists in being true to its own nature, and moving in its own sphere." (Robertson, *Sermons*, 3rd Series, 1857- 18 The First Miracle) (Robertson, *Sermons Preached at Brighton, by the late Rev. Frederick W. Robertson*, New York: Harper, 1905) p.395. (1860 onwards)

Mary's mind often skipped over the momentous and dwelled in the mundane; reference has already been made to her affinity for the 'ordinary' and the elevation of ordinary life in Christian practice. Again this is heavily reflected in religious literature:

"We are too fond of our own will. We want to be doing what we fancy mighty things; but the great point, is to do small things, when called to them, in a right spirit." (Cecil, R, *The Life and Remains of the Rev. Richard Cecil, 1854*) p.424. (London: Printed for Seeley, 1816). (3/28.9.1856)

"Christ was shown in little things. And such are the parts of human life. Opportunities for doing greatly seldom occur." (Robertson, *Sermons*, 1st Series, 1855- 16 The New Commandment of Love to One Another) (Robertson, *Sermons Preached at Brighton, by the late Rev. Frederick W. Robertson*, New York: Harper, 1905), p.182. (1860 onwards)

"Men have either gone out of the world, or sought to

render themselves 'and others miserable in it, just because they thought it necessary to "do some great thing in order to please God! ... what God looks for in us is, not the doing of some great thing, but the endeavour to be pure and holy in the performance of common duties and in the use of lawful enjoyments." (Vaughan, Lessons of life and Godliness, 1862) p.218.

"That a very ordinary lot, with very ordinary trials, may yet furnish a great field for the exercise of patience." (Boyd, The Graver Thoughts of a Country Parson, 2nd series, 1865) p.299. (Boston: Ticknor and Fields). (7/26.3.1865)

"The same God who has sent us His Word equally sends us the daily occurrences of life." (Goulburn, Thoughts on Personal Religion, 1864) p.195. (7/12.8.1866)

"They shew us that there is an eternal significance in our daily struggles, failures, attainments, and that there is a goal for all being." (Westcott, The Historic Faith, 1883) p.152. (1885). (13/30.3.1884)

"Little kindnesses are of enormous value." (Momerie, Preaching and Hearing, 1888) p.152. (1890). (15/20.10.1889)

"Not what I have done, not what I have believed, not what I have achieved, but how I have discharged the common charities of life." (Drummond, The City Without a Church, 1893) p.62. (16/9.4.1893)

Closely related to the above is the notion of **duty** which was most often promoted, especially for women, in terms of the common requirements of everyday life. Mary was imbued through and through with the necessity of observing duty, her duty as wife and mother, her duty to her household and estate servants, and even her duty to be cheerful. This attitude was much supported in many of the texts she read:

> *"Time may be owed ever so entirely as a duty at home; but the fragments belong to the poor, and we are bound to see that they have them."* (Sewell, *The Experience of Life*, 1853) p.135. (1858). (2/19.10.1853)

> *The two things which God hath joined together- duty and sunshine.* (Gordon, *Work, or, Plenty to Do and How to Do It*, 1854) p.38. (3/2.9.1855)

> *"The first step in spirituality is to get a distaste for common duties. ... But the last and highest step in spirituality is made in feeling these common duties again to be divine and holy. ... the blessed, second childhood of Christian life."* (Robertson, *Sermons*, 2nd Series, 1855 - 14 The Early Development of Jesus) (Robertson, *Sermons Preached at Brighton by the late Rev. Frederick W. Robertson*, New York: Harper, 1905) p.362. (1860 onwards)

> *"Pleasant as duty honestly performed may be, still in this world we must sometimes toil on when we have little heart or strength for it."* (Boyd, *The Graver Thoughts of a Country*

Parson, 1865, Second series) p.266. (Boston: Ticknor and Fields). (7/26.3.1865)

"*Despise not little sins; they have ruined many a soul. Despise not little duties;*" (Goulburn, *Thoughts on Personal Religion*, 1864) p.253. (7/12.8.1866)

"*Let us always strive to do thoroughly the work which we find nearest to our hand; though we may think it small and trifling, it is not so in the sight of Him who made the dewdrop as well as the sun, and who looks not so much upon the thing we have to do, as upon the way and the spirit in which we do it.*" (Clodd, *The Childhood of the World*, 1876) p.55. (10/13.2.1877)

"*There is a vast difference between Christ's way and the world's way of treating the individual. The duties which the imitation of Christ entails upon us are to be kind and unselfish in our family circles, to strive habitually to look on all men at their best, to write all our own wrongs in water and in ashes, and let them be to us as though they had never been.*" (Farrar, *Social and Present Day Questions*, 1892) p.69. (15/22.5.1892)

The longstanding controversy over the relative necessity of **faith and works** did not phase Mary; she focused on prayer and her personal relationship with Christ, but she also tried to manifest her Christianity in good works. Compassionate responses came naturally to her. Like Martha in the gospel story, she was active to help others, but as Mary (her namesake) she listened and contemplated. The texts she read provide various perspectives on this:

> "God does not want our work, Sally, but He does want our will. When we give it, we give all; when we withhold it, we give nothing." (Sewell, *The Experience of Life*, 1853) p.59. (1858). (2/19.10.1853)

> "Both St. Paul and St. James agree in the necessity of good works, springing from faith; but the justification of the ungodly does not spring from any worthiness, either in our faith or in our works." (Jowett, *The Christian Visitor*, 1841) p.119. (1836). (3/13.5.1855)

> "Perfection is being, not doing; it is not to effect an act, but to achieve a character." (Robertson, *Sermons*, 1st Series, 1855 - 4 *Christian Progress by Oblivion of the Past*) (Robertson, *Sermons Preached at Brighton, by the late Rev. Frederick W. Robertson*, New York: Harper, 1905) p.61. (1860 onwards)

> "By the deeds of the law shall no man living be justified. Salvation is by faith: a state of heart right with God; faith is the spring of holiness- a well of life. Salvation is not the having committed a certain number of good acts. Destruction is not the having committed a certain number of crimes. Salvation is God's spirit in us leading to good. Destruction is the selfish spirit in us, leading to wrong." (Robertson, *Sermons*, 3rd Series, 1857 - 19 *The Lawful and Unlawful Use of Law. A Fragment*) (Robertson, *Sermons Preached at Brighton, by*

the late Rev, Frederick W. Robertson, New York: Harper, 1905), p.600. (1860 onwards)

"Work, true work, done honestly and manfully for Christ, never can be a failure." (Robertson, Sermons, 3rd Series, 1857 - 21 John's Rebuke of Herod) (Robertson, Sermons Preached at Brighton, by the late Rev. Frederick W. Robertson, New York: Harper, 1905) pp.622-623. (1860 onwards)

"But we cannot forget how decided was His preference of that faith which sat at His feet and heard His word, over that activity which spent itself, root and branch, in deeds of bustling service." (Vaughan, Lessons of Life and Godliness, 1862) p.371. (Lessons of Life and Godliness and Words from the Gospels, 1891). (6/9.11.1862)

"We are saved by his work, not by our works." (Rundle, Chronicles of the Schönberg-Cotta Family, 1864) pp.271-272. (7/5.8.1864)

"Just in proportion to the degree to which you cease to think of self, and with a single eye make your Master's glory your great end, will be the good you will do." (Boyd, The Graver Thoughts of a Country Parson. 2nd Series, 1865) pp.51-52. (Boston: Ticknor and Fields). (7/26.3.1865)

"Surely faith is not a work. On the contrary, it is a ceasing from work. It is not a climbing of the mountain, but a ceasing to attempt it, and allowing Christ to carry you up in his own arms." (Reid, *The Blood of Jesus*, 1863) p.67. (1860). (7/ 3.9.1865)

"It is true that the good man does good deeds, but it is not necessarily true that he who does good deeds is a good man." (Seeley, *Ecce Homo*, 1866) p.67. (Boston: Roberts). (7/2.5.1866)

"In almost all cases the great, the permanent work has been done, not by those who seemed to do very much, but by those who seemed to do very little." (Temple, *Sermons Preached in Rugby School Chapel in 1862-1867*, 1871) p.139. (26.3.1871)

"It is the motive, as we all know, that more than anything else renders an action good or bad." (Hare, A., *The Alton Sermons*, 1878) p.327. (1874). (11 /1.12.1878)

"How many his occupations whom the world 'calls idle,' might be easily reversed. How great his idleness whom the world calls busy." (Stanley, *Memoirs of Edward and Catherine Stanley*, 1880) pp.222-223. (12/27.2.1880)

"It is a great thing to save life," she said. "To save a soul alive, how much greater! To have kept one soul in the knowledge that there is goodness, tenderness, mercy, God; to have given it bread to eat where it sat upon the stones, water to drink where all the streams were dry, - oh a king might be proud of that!- And that is what you have done for me..." (Johnston, *Audrey*, n.d.) p.244. (15/24.3.1891)

"*Though not by any number of formal actions can we enter into eternal life, yet no work done from a right motive, however erroneous, can be the fruit of an utterly corrupted tree ... Though no giving shall purchase interest in heaven, yet the poorest and slightest act which has sprung from a true charity- the kindly word spoken in Christ's name, the cup of cold water given for His sake,- shall not miss its reward.*" (Farrar, *The Silence and the Voices of God*, 1881) pp. 101-102. (New York: Dutton, 1874). (15/3.5.1891)

"*Yet inaction need not be uselessness. The land that lies fallow under the winter frost is mellowing for the spring sowing. It is very possible to be useless amid a great deal of fussy and showy activity, and to be seeking the praise of men, not of God. If we are bringing forth the fruits of the Spirit, we are not useless.*" (Thorold, *The Presence of Christ*, 1889) p.121. (New York: Randolph, 1880). (15/1.11.1891)

An emphasis of **heart over intellect** was both instinctive to Mary and integral to her outlook. Her Christian lovingness is manifest throughout the diaries and well exemplified in her warmth towards Lindsey, her half-brother, the mentally challenged heir to the Lindsey title. She loved him for no gain, with humour and infinite patience, whilst others regarded him as a burden. Mary referred to a sermon *full of warm hearty practical Christianity -& sound doctrine* (3/7.5.1854) and another *full of good Christian feeling* (3/6.8.1854), demonstrating her relationship with Christianity through the heart rather than through intellect, and this links with a sense, explored in the next chapter, that the knowledge of Christ was primarily experiential and intuitive rather than arising from fact or reason. Many texts underline the importance of the heart:

> "The heart must be offered withal, and the whole heart, all of it entirely given to him." (Leighton, *A Practical Commentary upon the First Epistle of St. Peter*, 1845) p.250. (Bohn, 1849). (1/30.8.1846)

> "I do not desire that my imagination should dwell too much on spiritual things; for the real work of religion is in the heart." (Timpson, *Memoirs of Mrs Elizabeth Fry*, 1847) p.308. (1/6.3.1848)

> "Man is to be made one with God, not by soaring intellect, but by lowly love." (Robertson, *Sermons*, 3rd Series, 1857 - 4 The Trinity) (Robertson, *Sermons Preached at Brighton, by the late Rev. Frederick W. Robertson*, New York: Harper, 1905) p.475. (1860 onwards)

> "He secures the heart; and when that is won, all is won." (Rundle, *Chronicles of the Schönberg-Cotta Family*, 1864) p.340. (7/5.8.1864)

> "Truth is felt, not reasoned out." (Robertson; Brooke, *Life and letters of Frederick W. Robertson*, 1865) vol 2, p.42. (7/19.11.1865)

Some of the writers Mary read were clearly imbued with the notion of original sin:

> "The germ of faith is latent in every child's soul, but beside it lies the poisonous seed of sin." (Poel, *Life of Amelia Wilhelmina Sieveking*, 1863) p.147. (6/2.1.1864)

> "Little Augustus is in an ecstasy of delight over all the primroses and daffodils that cover our hedges and fields. But it is surprising even in a child how many seeds of evil show themselves before they have had time to develop themselves fully." (Hare, *Memorials of a Quiet Life*, 1873) p.202. (1872). (9/21.8.1873)

Charles Kingsley, embracing the need for approaching religion as a child, expressed a much more benign view of the state of childhood:

> "If I was born honest, and strong, and gentle, and brave, some one must have made me so when I was born, or before." (Kingsley, *Twenty-five Village Sermons*, 1854). p.33. (1857). (9/14.1.1856)

It was appropriate and blessed to approach religion like a child.

> "We never pray aright except when we pray in that feminine childlike spirit which no logic can defend, feeling as if we modified the will of God, though that will is fixed."

(Robertson, *Sermons*, 2nd Series, 1855 - 17 *The First Miracle*) (Robertson, *Sermons Preached at Brighton, by the late Rev. Frederick Robertson*, New York: Harper, 1905) p.386. (1860 onwards)

> "The kingdom of a perfect song, the kingdom of a perfect work of art, is like the kingdom of heaven, one must enter it like a little child." (Brooke, *Christ in Modern Life*, 1880) p.286. (New York: Appleton, 1877). (12/16.11.1880)

> "The condition of entrance into the spiritual kingdom is to possess the child-spirit-that state of mind combining at once the profoundest helplessness with the most artless feeling of dependence." (Drummond, *Natural Law in the Spiritual World*, 1883) p.271. (New York: Pott, 1884). (13/13.7.1884)

Mary similarly appeared to regard childhood as innocent and corruption to come from the world rather than from within. She spoke thus of some children who were dancing **after a natural fashion of their own:**

> Something affecting to seeing them move with light hearts & light feet- & I earnestly desired for them that they might so bound unshackled by the weight of sin & sorrow which the world too surely brings as its portion & may they set the Lord always before them, so shall they not be moved. (2/3.9.1851)

The childlike approach in Christianity was not only often

recommended in literature, but was also scriptural and it is characteristic also of Mary herself, although she doesn't talk much about this. Her attitude was mysteriously simple. A woman of high intelligence, as evidenced by the substance of her reading and conversations, she nonetheless conformed, apparently without much question, to the Christian religion of her upbringing, though embracing the modifications that came with respected and clerical opinions. In reading and conversation she generally gave more evidence of listening than of offering criticism or participating loudly. Complexity may have characterised her thoughts but did not enter her religious attitudes.

One strongly evangelical doctrine was the **importance of Scripture**, often read in a fundamental way, though there were differences of opinion on interpretation, especially as regards the merits of reading the text as poetry or allegory. Scripture was highly important to Mary and she noted the readings in Church every Sunday, and often perused the Bible at home with husband or children. How she interpreted Scripture and what were her views on Heaven and Hell are not clear for she read disparate opinions on these and commented little. The vital role of Scripture is emphasised in many of the texts she read:

> "I dare to assert that I yield to no man in firm belief that all Scripture is given by inspiration; but, then, given only for the purposes specified, viz. 'for doctrine, for reproof etc... I am equally satisfied that proofs have been established, by arguments conclusive to all who have learnt to appreciate the evidence, that the inspired writers were often left to convey

their lessons in their own words, intelligible to those whom they addressed, and in accordance with their own imperfect or erroneous views of nature." (Jenyns, Memoir of the Rev. John Stevens Henslow, 1862) p.217. (26.7.1863)

"In the text we find two principles: first, that Scripture is of universal application; and second, that all the lines of Scripture converge towards Jesus Christ." (Robertson, Sermons, 4th Series, 1863- 28 Inspiration) (Robertson, Sermons Preached at Brighton, by the late Rev. Frederick W. Robertson, New York: Harper, 1905) p.826. (1860 onwards)

"What matters it, whether the story be literal or allegorical, so long as we believe in Jesus and his tomb, and know that He rose from it triumphantly?" (Hare, A., Memorials of a Quiet Life, 1873) p.340. (1872). (9/21.8.1873)

"The question which forces itself upon all who are interested in the education of the young, is what they shall be taught regarding the relation of the Bible to other sacred scriptures, and to the declarations of modern science where they fail to harmonise with its statements." (Clodd, The Childhood of Religions, 1876). p.iii. (Kegan Paul, 1883). (11/4.2.1877)

"The first victory of Protestantism was the right to read the Bible, the next must be the right to interpret it." (Reid, The Life, Letters and Friendships of Richard Monckton Milnes, 1891) vol 2, p.493. (15/6.6.1891)

"Many utterances in the Bible of this description relate to a totally different state of affairs from any existing among ourselves." (Oliphant, M., *Memoir of the Life of Laurence Oliphant*, 1891) p.282. (New York: Harper). (15/29.8.1891)

Mary's thoughts dwelled increasingly on the life to come, though she did not make many direct references to **Heaven** and none to **Hell**. As a fourteen year-old, describing with sadness the plight of a poor old woman living contentedly in a hovel from which she would soon be evicted, she declared, *Wishes are not for this world but for the next.* (15.9.1836). The drowning of her sister in 1837 evoked the following comments: *My dearest sister Elizabeth was drowned & is now an angel in heaven! She cannot come to me but I shall, I hope join her in those realms of blue, from which she is now looking down upon us.* (5.4.1837); *Yes- she certainly is now in Paradise, calmly awaiting the day of Resurrection.* (8.4.1837). Strangely she talked of Heaven soon after her wedding, probably because of a state of heightened emotion at this time: *I thought much on the happiness of Heaven & wish (?) a more perfect knowledge of the wonders & mysteries of creation, be included among the joys of the just, in a state of glory.* (1/26.5.1844)

Heaven and Hell and the eternal were all much spoken of in religious literature and the examples below are mixed, since references to both often appeared together. They also embrace a wide variety of perceptions of this topic:

"Rose knew there were two worlds beyond the grave, one the only heaven, and another the dreadful hell." (Charlesworth,

Ministering Children, 1854) p.31. (New York: Riker, 1855). (3/4.9.1855)

"Nothing that dies perishes to nothing, but begins a new and a higher life." (Kingsley, *Twenty-five Village Sermons*, 1854) p.27. (1857). (3/14.1.1856)

"If any one asks, what is a man, the true answer is an animal with an immortal spirit in it; but a man's spirit, on the other hand, if it be in hell, is in a very different hell from mere fire, - a spiritual hell, such as torments the evil spirits, at this very moment, although they are going to and fro on this very earth. This earth is hell to them; they carry about hell in them, - they are their own hell." (Kingsley, *Twenty-five Village Sermons*, 1854) pp. 57/58 (1857). (3/14.1.1856)

"All places are heaven, if you will be heavenly in them. Heaven is where God is." (Kingsley, *Twenty-five Village Sermons*, 1854) p.198. (1857). (3/14.1.1856)

"We may form some idea of the joys of heaven, by the innocent pleasures which God grants us on earth." (Cecil, *The life and Remains of the Rev. Richard Cecil*, 1854) p.437. (London: Printed for Seeley, 1816). (3/28.9.1856)

"The wicked will not be able to get away. They will burn for ever and ever." (Mortimer, *The Peep of Day*, 1849) p.200. (4/10.5.1857)

"The anguish of the lost ones of this world is not fear of punishment. It was, and is, the misery of having quenched a light brighter than the sun: the intolerable sense of being sunk: the remorse of knowing that they were not what they might have been." (Robertson, *Sermons*, 2nd Series, 1855 - 15 Christ's Estimate of Sin) (Robertson, *Sermons Preached at Brighton, by the late Rev. Frederick W. Robertson*, New York: Harper, 1905) p.369. (1860 onwards)

"That a system of pleasure and pains has been annexed to virtue and vice, of such a character that virtue is made its own reward, and vice its own punishment." (Farrar, *Science in Theology*, 1859) p.31. (5/24. 3.1861)

"The whole world is one grand demonstration of life to encourage us in the sure conviction of life eternal." (Jenyns, *Memoir of the Rev. John Stevens Henslow*, 1862) p.257. (6/26.7.1863)

"It is a necessity to me, to believe in the progressive education of man after death." (Poel, *Life of Amelia Wilhelmina Sieveking*, 1863) p.202. (6/2.1.1864)

"The final day of judgment may be millions of years hence. ... Many picture a heaven which is a reflection of their own selfish nature." (Macleod, *Memoir of Norman Macleod*, 1876) vol 1, p.407. (New York: Worthington). (10/15.4.1876)

"Kingsley enabled me to dismiss at once and for ever all

faith whatever in the popular doctrine of eternal punishment, and all the whole class of dogmas which tend to confuse the characters of God and the Devil." (Kingsley, *Charles Kingsley: His Letters and Memories of His Life*, 1877) vol 1, p.228. (11/1.4.1877)

"Love is Heaven, and Heaven is Love." (Stanley, *Memoirs of Edward and Catherine Stanley*, 1880) p.148. (12/27.2.1880)

"Nor does Christianity appeal to fear of punishment, but to the feeling of love." (Brooke, *Christ in Modern Life*, 1880) p.167. (New York: Appleton,1877). (12/16.11.1880)

"The eternal life is not future: it is, it is now. It lies in a relation to God through Christ." (Westcott, *Historic Faith*, 1883) p.146. (13/30.3.1884)

"It is not said that the character will develop in all its fulness in this life." (Drummond, *Natural Law in the Spiritual World*, 1883) p.129. (New York: Pott, 1884). (13/13.7.1884)

"Why is it that the Christian fears death? Because he has had preached to him a gospel of Damnation instead of a gospel of Salvation." (Davies, *Orthodox London*, 1876) p.15. (1874). (13/30.11.1884)

"There is a harvest of character that follows from human actions; and this is at once the most important, the most *certain, and the most unavoidable form of retribution. The place a man goes to in the future, as in the present, is emphatically his own place- the place for which by his conduct he has prepared himself."* (Momerie, Preaching and Hearing, 1888) p.294. (1890). (15/20.10.1889)

"You must choose now in this life, you cannot choose hereafter when you die." (Lonsdale, Sister Dora, 1888) p.147. (1881). (15/21.11.1889)

"To love abundantly is to live abundantly, and to love for ever is to live for ever. Hence, eternal life is inextricably bound up with love." (Drummond, The Greatest Thing in the World 1890) p.57. (15/9.4.1890)

"The life-lesson which Christ said He meant to teach was watchfulness; the misery which the want of watchfulness entailed was exclusion." (Benson, Living Theology, 1891) p.182. (1893). (15/28.1.1892)

"He is a besetting God; He is a pervading God. If we go into heaven, He is there; if we go down into hell, He is there also." (Farrar, Social and Present Day Questions, 1892) p.136. (15/22.5.1892)

"Then pass out into the City. Do all to it that you have done at home. ... By far the greatest thing a man can do for his City is to be a good man." (Drummond, The City Without a Church, 1893) pp.25-26. (16/9.4.1893)

> "The only preparation which multitudes seem to make for Heaven is for its Judgment Bar. What will they do in its streets? Earth is the rehearsal for Heaven." (Drummond, *The City Without a Church*, 1893) p.53. (6/9.4.1893)

Mary steadfastly believed in the value of suffering to hasten the approach to God's Kingdom, according to her spiritual understanding of God's Chastening and its counterpart, God's Providence. Every time fate dealt her a blow, such as the death of her husband, the loss of child, the loss of land, she brought the idea of chastening into play using it as a form of self-discipline and also of bitter comfort. Whilst there were joyful times, especially in the earlier years, progress was generally measured in the patient bearing of adversity. There would, in any case, be little other sense to make of the relentless decline. As her spirituality grew, so her concerns for material life lessened:

> *Perhaps to us of all others this last year has been one of trial. How comforting is the text 'The Lord loveth whom he chasteneth'.* (the year Mary's sister drowned) (31.12.1837)

> *He who sustains us by his love from day to day, only withdraws his countenance for a little moment to bring our own wandering hearts back to Him, on whom we are dependant for His smallest mercies.* (1/6.8.1846)

> *God only chastises me- & that the very least of His chastisements would be withheld? Would I remain in safety*

without it? I prayed more for the healing of my soul - & that it would please God to make this the prevailing feeling of my mind. At present it is but as a meteor in a dark night, but I would implore the Lord that it may never be thoroughly eclipsed until the dayspring in my heart even the Sun of Righteousness arises (omission) with healing on his wings. (1/12.8.1846)

W.B. preached upon God's voice proclaimed in the events of the world as in the cholera. (2/9.10.1853)

But we must learn to bow to God's will (on sale of Aboyne Castle). (14/14.7.1887)

Read a sermon of Robertson in which he speaks of the true character as a reflection of the Divine & this may be applied to dear Douglas. ... May we bow to God's will. (12/12.8.1888)

Dear D's birthday- Oh! to say from the heart 'Thy will be done'. (15/11.10.1889) (regarding the death of Douglas)

Again, this response to adversity was continually reflected in Mary's reading:

"*Whom the Lord loveth he chasteneth.*" (Timpson, *Memoirs of Mrs Elizabeth Fry*, 1847) p.51. (1854). (1/6.3.1848)

"*It would be most melancholy, to have no afflictions: if we* had none, we might then doubt whether we were the children of God; for what son is he, whom the father chasteneth not." (Jowett, *The Christian Visitor*, 1836) p.137. (3/13.5.1855)

"How blessed is the Christian in the midst of his greatest troubles!" (Cecil; Pratt, *The Life and Remains of the Rev. Richard Cecil*, 1854) p.450. (London, Printed for Seeley, 1816). (3/28.9.1856)

"By this I mean that men are placed in a condition for the trial and discipline of their characters, in order to fit them for a higher state." (Hitchcock, *The Religion of Geology*, 1856) p.246. (Boston, Phillips; Sampson, 1857). (3/29.9.1856)

"Never does a man know the force that is in him till some mighty affection or grief has humanized the soul." (Robertson, Sermons, 2nd Series, 1855- 18 *The First Miracle*) (Robertson, *Sermons Preached at Brighton, by the late Rev. Frederick W. Robertson*, New York: Harper, 1905) p.401. (1860 onwards)

"God sends the famine into the soul- the hunger, and thirst, and the disappointment- to bring back his erring child again." (Robertson, *Sermons* 3rd Series, 1857- 20 *The Prodigal and His Brother*) (Robertson, *Sermons Preached at Brighton, by the late Rev. Frederick W. Robertson*, New York: Harper, 1905) p.608. (1860 onwards)

"It is generally in a way of chastisement that God instructs."

(Bateman, *The Life of the Right Rev. Daniel Wilson*, 1860) p.214. (5/15.7.1860)

"But I do believe that God is still over all, and that everything is working for good. These things are the fire and water through which this nation must pass." (Trollope, *North America*, 1862) vol 1, p.384. (New York: Harper). (6/9.11.1863)

"And the text tells us that a life of unbroken ease, a life in which all goes well with us, is a most perilous thing." (Boyd, *The Graver Thoughts of a Country Parson*, 2nd Series, 1865) p.22. (Boston: Ticknor and Fields). (7/26.3.1865)

"The education, for instance, of the character and heart through pain;" (Robertson, F. W.; S. A. Brooke, *Life and letters of Frederick W. Robertson*, 1865). vol, 2, p.47. (7/19.11.1865)

"But because we are not to hate an enemy, it does not immediately follow that we are not to take vengeance upon him. The infliction of pain and damage is quite consistent with love, as we all acknowledge in the instance of a parent punishing a child." (Seeley, *Ecce Homo*, 1866) p.326. (Boston: Roberts). (7/2.5.1866)

"Every thing of this kind happens by the permission of One who watches over us with most tender care; and this may turn out for the best." (Livingstone; Horace, *The Last Journals of*

David Livingstone in Central Africa, 1874) vol 1, p.178. (10/6.12.1875)

"Much sorrow must belong to man ere he can receive much joy." (Macleod, *Memoir of Norman Macleod*, 1876) vol 1, p.210. (New York: Worthington). (10/15.4.1876)

"Sickness, in his eyes, seemed always to sanctify and purify." (Kingsley, *Charles Kingsley: His Letters and Memories of His Life*, 1877) vol 1, p.227.4. (11/1.4.1877)

"The redeeming quality of personal infirmity is that it brings its special duty with it; but this privilege waits long to be recognised." (Martineau; Chapman, *Harriet Martineau's Autobiography*, 1877). vol 1, p.95. (Boston, Osgood). (11/15.5.1877)

"It is doubtless for some wise purpose we have been kept in scarceness among runagates and spendthrifts." (Besant, *The Chaplain of the fleet*, 1887) p.100. (1888). (14/1.9.1887)

"Now the child cannot see the wisdom of a parent's severity." (Davies, *Orthodox London*, 1876) p.13. (1874). (13/30.11.1884)

"He advocated the blending of humanity with justice, and looked upon the sufferings of a culprit as chastisement to be administered in mercy." (Stoughton, *Howard the Philanthropist and His Friends*, 1884) p.338. (13/28.12.1884)

> "Those bitter times of religious dryness and hopelessness, by which God chastens from time to time His most faithful and heroic souls." (Ward, *Robert Elsmere*, 1888) p.326. (Smith, Elder). (15/3.12.1888)

> "He sends sorrow to draw our souls nearer to Him." (Deland, *John Ward, Preacher*, 1889) p.163. (Boston; New York: Houghton, Mifflin, 1888). (15/31.5.1889)

> "But chastisement is sent not only to recall the backslider, or to set the mark of God's displeasure on some act or habit of sin; it is to sanctify us, to add to our personal and positive holiness, to edify us higher into the image of Christ." (Thorold, *The Presence of Christ*, 1889) p.97. (New York: Randolph, 1880) (15/1.11.1891)

For Mary, just as trials were from God, so were good things. For example, ***The bright blue sky & fresh buoyant air forcibly reminded me of the ever-existing goodness of God & of the very many blessings one of the least deserving of his creatures is permitted to enjoy.*** (23.10.1841); ***Received the news of the termination of the entail case in Strath's favour. Thanked God for the good news.*** (1/8.9.1844)

Mary also read much of the benign gifts of Providence:

> "Providence makes nothing that lives, to live quite alone." (Cooper, *The Pathfinder*, 1840). p.283. (New York: Hurd and Houghton, 1877). (20.5.1841)

"*Every good gift we have comes from Him; but He will have us know where they all come from*" (Kingsley, *Twenty-five Village Sermons*, 1854) p.34. (1857). (3/14.1.1856)

"*No success or failure in such speculations could vitally affect our belief in a wise and benevolent Deity: - that though additional illustrations of his attributes might be interesting and welcome, no change of our scientific point of view could make his being or action doubtful.*" (Whewell, *Of the Plurality of Worlds*, 1855) p.216. (1853). (3/3.3.1856)

"*Compare such a world with that now teeming with life, and beauty, and glory, which we inhabit; and say, must not the transition to its present condition have demanded the exercise of infinite power, infinite wisdom, and infinite benevolence.*" (Hitchcock, *Religion of Geology*, 1856) p.164. (Boston, Phillips; Sampson, 1857). (3/29.9.1856)

"*We should work like the bees, sedulous to collect all the honey within our reach, but leaving to Providence to order what shall come of it. The good which our exertions effect may rarely, or never, become visible.*" (Grindon, *Life: Its Nature, Varieties, and Phenomena*, 1856) p.91. (3/11.11.1856)

"*To solve the question to his heart which still perplexes us through life - the co-existence of evil with Divine benevolence.*" (Robertson, *Sermons*, 4th Series, 1863 - 14 *Salvation out of the Visible Church*) (Robertson, *Sermons Preached at*

Brighton, by the late Rev. Frederick W. Robertson, New York: Harper, 1905) p.723. (1860 onwards)

"It is not merely in the benevolence of a growing civilisation that we notice the merciful arrangements of Heaven for the mitigation of pain; we trace it much more in the mission of Christianity." (Farrar, Science in Theology, 1859) p.93. (5/24.3.1861)

"That there is a meaning in everything that happens to us; in everything, small and great." (Boyd, The Graver Thoughts of a Country Parson, 2nd Series, 1865) p.20. (Boston: Ticknor and Fields). (7/26.3.1865)

"The true wisdom is to see in all the steps of this earth's progress the guiding hand of God, and to believe that He will not leave to itself the world which for His own pleasure He has created." (Clodd, The Childhood of the World, 1876) p.55. (11/13.2.1877)

"But of one thing you may be assured, that unseen beings care for you, and that nothing can happen to you without the permission of our heavenly Father." (Smiles, Robert Dick, 1878) p.347. (11/30.12.1878)

"The exhibition of Divine power and goodness in the natural world" (Stanley; Stanley, Memoirs of Edward and Catherine Stanley, 1880) p.15. (12/27.2.1880)

"Yet it is also to be observed that few evils are altogether unmixed. God, contemplating apparently the unbending action of his great laws, has established others which appear to be designed to have a compensating, a repairing, and a consoling effect." (Chambers, Vestiges of the Natural History of Creation, 1884) p.277. (Routledge, 1887). (13/10.2.1885)

Mary, even at the darkest times, could contemplate good prevailing over evil: **Chimes ringing in New Year melancholy. Most of the family were dancing at Orton a year ago! May all trials sent by God work together for our good.** (14/31.12.1885); **The Prospects for the poor child** (Mary's grandchild Beatrice was, she felt, suffering in an atmosphere of domestic disharmony) **are very sad. God alone can over rule all for good.** (15/9.10.1889)

4

The Books: Questioning Faith

The anguish of despair which comes when a soul feels itself adrift upon a sea of unbelief.
(Deland, *John Ward, Preacher*, 1889) p.141. (Boston: Houghton, Mifflin, 1888) (15/31.5.1889)

We must love before we can see but the dissecting analyzing spirit of the day- destroys the object & only thinks it sees.
Mary's Diaries (11/19.5.1878)
(Written after hearing a sermon of Stopford Brook at Bedford Chapel, Woburn Place Bloomsbury: 'Open thou mine eyes that I may behold wondrous things out of thy law.')

Mary showed herself impressed by the anti-rationalist message conveyed by this sermon, reflecting the fact that, although she was capable of a scholarly and scientific approach, her first responses to life's forms and events were instinctively emotional and spiritual. The first quotation, refers not to Mary, whose faith, it seems, was never in question, but to the many who lost their religious certainty.

The nineteenth century has been widely characterised as a period of religious upheaval and scepticism, usually attributed to questionings about the accuracy and authenticity of the Bible and the growth of scientific theories and discoveries which appeared to contradict Scripture, including those of Charles Darwin; also to the break-up of community and feelings of alienation due to increasing industrialisation and urbanisation in the latter part of the century. The extracts below from texts read by Mary document the spiritual chaos of her times and the threat from forces sceptical to religion and to the hopes of immortality which are associated with Christianity. (The views quoted from characters in fictional works, both in this section and other sections of this chapter, do not, of course, necessarily represent the views of the authors of those works.)

> *"In this we cannot be mistaken that an open and professed disregard to religion is become, through a variety of unhappy causes, the distinguishing character of the present age, that Christianity is now ridiculed and railed at with very little*

reserve, and the teachers of it without any at all." (Bickersteth, *The Works of Rev E. Bickersteth*, 1832) p.272. fn. (*A Scripture Help*, London: s.n.,1852). (16.6.1837)

"This union of vice and intellectual power and knowledge seems to me rather a sign of the age; and if it goes on, it threatens to produce one of the most fearful forms of Antichrist which has yet appeared." (Arnold; Stanley, *The Life and Correspondence of Thomas Arnold*, 1846) vol 1, p.67. (1844). (1/3.12.1847)

"I have had a conversation with our new friend, which, considering his relative situation, gives me serious concern. I find that he is an unbeliever, that he has filled his memory with every trite, pert, and often confuted argument against the character of the Bible, beginning with the Creation, and ending with the most solemn and sublime of our doctrines." (Trench, *The Remains of the Late Mrs. Richard Trench*, 1862) p.391. (6/25.9.1862)

"Few days since, I read a review of a book by an American author, the purpose of which book is to show that this creation never had any Creator, and that this universe goes on somehow by itself without any Providence to direct it. Various learned, able, wrong-headed, and bad-hearted men have, of late years, set out the like dismal doctrine." (Boyd, *The Graver Thoughts of a Country Parson*, Series 2 1865) p.18. (Boston Ticknor & Fields, 1865). (7/26.3.1865)

"We live under the blessed light of science, a light yet far from its meridian and dispersing every day some noxious superstition, some cowardice of the human spirit." (Seeley, Ecce Homo, 1866) p.353. (Boston, Roberts). (7/2.5.1866)

"In the present day philosophy and science stand aloof in unfriendly attitudes, whilst literature gives currency to a thousand speculative opinions unfavourable to the old established beliefs." (Somerset, Christian Theology and Modern Scepticism, 1872) pp.3-4. (9/12.4.1872)

"Turn from the laity to the Church, and note the state of excitement in which it lives. No well-known teachers of any party can speak on any religious subject without awaking a quite disproportioned excitement." (Brooke, Sermons Preached in St. James's Chapel, 1871) p.159. (London: King, 1871). (4/18.7.1873)

"That the strongest mental power, the finest thought, the highest intelligence among us, is yearly diverging more and more from Christianity, is discarding all faith in it, assuming towards it not so much a hostile, as an isolated, neutral, almost supercilious, attitude- an attitude which may perhaps best be described as one of silent renunciation and disapproval- of looking, and 'passing by on the other side.'" (Greg, Rocks Ahead, 1874) p.128. (10/6.3.1875)

"I am more and more painfully awake to the fact that the curse of our generation is that so few of us deeply believe *anything. Men dally with truth, and with lies. They deal in innuendoes, impersonalities, conditionalities; they have no indicative mood - no I, no thou - whereby alone have any great souls conquered."* (Kingsley; Charles Kingsley: His Letters and Memories of His Life, 1877). vol 1, pp.140-141. (11/1.4.1877)

"The present writer remembers how, while waiting for him in his library, he found a pile of the newest sceptical books and reviews upon his table, with each salient passage in their arguments underlined, and commented on in the margin." (Ashwell; Wilberforce, Life of the Right Reverend Samuel Wilberforce, 1883) p.xx. (New York: Dutton, 1883). (13/12.10.1883)

"The religious inconsistencies of Christendom are pressing themselves so forcibly on the more enlightened minds and quickened consciences of the present day, that we see ourselves involved in a reaction against the popular theology, which, unfortunately, finds its expression in materialism, agnosticism, positivism, and other philosophical attempts at the solution of the social and moral problem." (Oliphant, Altiora Peto, 1883) p.271. (1884). (13/27.11.1883)

"There could be no rest until all was clear to the intellect. God was made hideous by a dreadful theology, and the love of God being gone, only thirst for knowledge remained; but intellect could not touch these questions. And yet this was the common position of educated men. It was nothing less than a mutilation of their humanity. The only remedy was

a teaching of theology which would enable men to love god again." (Davies, *Orthodox London*, 1876) p.215. (1874). (13/ 30.11.1884)

"*Revealed religion is on its trial before the world, not for some trifling blemishes which a little mild correction may mend, but for its very life.*" (Pullen, *Modern Christianity*, 1884) p.3. (Boston, Gill, 1875). (14/19.1.1886)

"*We have lived to see the sun shine out of an empty heaven, to light up a soul-less earth: we have felt with utter loneliness, that the Great Companion is dead.*" (Curteis, *The Scientific Obstacles to Christian Belief*, 1885) p.36. (quoting Professor Clifford, Essays ii. 247). (15/5.7.1889)

"*Hope, faith, and God seemed impossible amidst the smoke of the streets.*" (William Hale White, *The Autobiography of Mark Rutherford*, 1889) p.149. (15/5.9.1889)

"*Similarly, it has been maintained that we have no spirit, no faculty for discerning God; that religion is nothing but the fanaticism of an undisciplined intellect. We cannot open a magazine, we can hardly take up a newspaper, without statements of this kind staring us in the face.*" (Momerie, *Preaching and Hearing*, 1888) p.115. (1890). (15/20.10.1889)

"*In this age of criticism nothing is too sacred to be questioned and investigated, and the present generation is accustomed to see the most vital questions connected with the*

Bible discussed with the utmost freedom." (Smyth, *The Old Documents and the New Bible*, 1890) p.v. (15/17.12.1891)

"And I have been doing it all my time here- morally, spiritually, as well as materially, digging the church out of the smothering sands, and all in vain- all profitless work." (Baring-Gould, *In The Roar of the Sea*, 1892) vol 1, p.7. (16/20.11.1892)

This did not necessarily persist as a shocking state of affairs, but could begin to seem socially acceptable and could even be discussed lightheartedly.

"When Mr. Alleyne found that his pupil was, as he termed it, 'a thorough-going young atheist,' he was a little amused and a good deal interested." (Lyall, *Donovan*, 1882) vol 1, p.43. (14/21.4.1887)

"The day has passed for forcing people into believing things" (Deland, *John Ward, Preacher*, 1889) p.324. (Boston: Houghton, Mifflin,1888). (15/31.5.1889)

The increasing friction between science and religion during the century, especially in the years following the publication of some of Darwin's major works, impacted on Mary's reading and thought processes. In 1860 she wrote: **We** (she and Strath) **had some interesting conversation upon Darwin's Origin of Species.** (5/15.2.1860). She reported reading this work less than a month later (5/6.3.1860) and, after a decade, read the *Descent of Man*, (9/

22.3.1871) commenting a few days later that it **comprises a large collection of facts but no very clear solutions drawn from them.**(9/30.3.1871). These words seem non-committal in terms of Mary's response, though it is also possible that Darwin's work may have evoked conflict between her religious beliefs and scientific understanding. Mary was generally happy with the apologetic writings and she expressed particular appreciation of Chambers' *Vestiges of the Natural History of Creation* (1884) where, despite the startling scientific findings, she was able, as with many such works, to pick up the positives in what she read.

Chambers stated in his work:

> "This book, as far as I am aware, is the first attempt to connect the natural sciences into a history of creation." (Chambers; Ireland, *Vestiges of the Natural History of Creation*, 1884) p.284. (London: Routledge, 1887). (13/10.2.1885)

Mary wrote: **Finished reading Vestiges. I like the last chapter.** (13/11.2.1885)

She also read a good representation of controversial texts which were abundant at this time and, indeed, the breadth of her reading and extent of her discussions seems strangely at odds with the calm and uninterrupted regularity of her prayers, churchgoing and perusal of scriptures. However, if it ever appeared that she had a simple and narrow-minded approach to religion, this is belied by her ceaseless mental activity in exploring the field. She was interested in every denomination and every religious concept; she also read about nihilism, spiritualism, atheism, agnosticism and the endless disputes between clerics and scientists and Bible critics on fundamental questions of belief. She became acquainted with every shade of view, from complete contempt of religion to denial of new scientific discoveries and all the apologetics, and reconcilements and anguished questionings between the two.

One of her motivations in reading so much religious literature may have been to enhance her capacities as a religious teacher, primarily to her children but also to servants, working men and mothers' groups; another, especially in terms of the diversity of reading, to achieve an understanding and maintain a position in the many theological conversations that took place in her social circle, and to accommodate herself to the differing views of those close to her. A third and, perhaps, the most important reason was her own intellectual curiosity. She was open-minded to what she read though rarely persuaded away from her well-trodden pathways and beliefs but, whilst not 'owning up' to any doubts of her own, she seemed uncritical of those beset by doubts. Although Mary expressed warm feelings towards the supportive texts discussed in the last chapter, very few reactions to the more highly sceptical and controversial texts are recorded. Possibly she could read with interest but dismiss the cynical messages.

In fact, her strong objections seemed to arise more when her expectations of writers 'friendly' to her views seemed to be violated. This was particularly the case with the publication of

Natural Law in the Spiritual World by Henry Drummond who was, in fact, an acquaintance of hers and a fervent evangelist:

Drummond wrote in his introduction:

> "No class of works is received with more suspicion, I had almost said derision, than those which deal with Science and Religion. Science is tired of reconciliations between two things which never should have been contrasted; religion is offended by the patronage of an ally which it professes not to need; and the critics have rightly discovered that, in most cases where Science is either pitted against Religion or fused with it, there is some fatal misconception to begin with as to the scope and province of either." (Drummond, Natural Law in the Spiritual World, 1883) p. v. (New York: Pott, 1884). (13/13.7.1884)

He set out his thesis thus:

> "Is there not reason to believe that many of the Laws of the Spiritual World, hitherto regarded as occupying an entirely separate province, are simply the Laws of the Natural World?" (Drummond, Natural Law in the Spiritual World, 1883) p.vi. (New York: Pott, 1884). (13/13.7.1884)

He went on to elaborate on this theme, presenting Christianity as a landmark in evolution and consistent with its laws:

> "And the Reign of Law will transform the whole Spiritual

World as it has already transformed the Natural World." (Drummond, *Natural Law in the Spiritual World*, 1883) p.ix. (New York: Pott, 1884). (13/13.7.1884)

The book did, in fact, cause widespread controversy, and deeply upset Mary. Apart from its main argument which was that spiritual law mirrored the laws of nature and shared the same process of evolution, she may have been offended by some other elements, such as the description of churchgoing as a parasitic activity. She may also have felt that religion was here making far too much concession to science.

Later she returned to friendship with Drummond and was complimentary about his subsequent publications. Her diary tells the story as follows: **Read a theological book sent by John Layard** (13/13.7.1884); *Tried to analyse John Layard's* (written by Professor Drummond) *Natural Law in the spiritual world.* (13/21.7. 1884); *Long talk on theological subjects & the meanings of Mr Drummond's book.* (13/17.8.1884); *Had some theological talk with Mr Marsh.* (13/19.8.1884); *Marsh reading Natural Life etc and discussing different points.* (13/21.8.1884); *Read Robertson & looked over part of Professor Drummond's Book.* (13/8.2.1885); *Had a talk with the Canon about Professor Drummond's book in the condemnation of which he quite agrees with me. Brought away with me a forcible article on it by 'Prof Watson' entitled 'Professor Drummond's new Scientific Gospel;'* (13/21.3.1885); *Thinking over the arguments in Drummond's book.* (13/24.3.1885); *Walked with Mr. Marsh on my return. He read aloud the Article in the Contemporary Review on Professor Drummond's New Scientific Gospel.* (13/2.4.1885); *Wrote to*

John Layard on Professor D's theology & sent him the review of the book. (3/3.4.1885); Wrote to Johnson for a book entitled Biological Religion- a continuation of Drummond's Natural Law etc. (13/ 20.7.1885); Wrote to Professor Drummond. (14/ 9.6.1886); Read at night Drummond's pretty little book The Greatest Thing in the World Charity- not original but well put. (15/9.4.1890); Read a little book of Drummond's on Heaven as a city, not a church. (16/9.4.1893)

Mary had at least one other somewhat violent reaction to a work. This was *The Female Jesuit* by Jemima Luke, which she describes as *a horrid book.* (2/27.11.1851). The reason can only be guessed, though the manner in which the deceptively pious image of the main character was later turned on its head as she emerged as an impostor, could have seemed particularly evil to the devoted Mary.

The analysis below, supported by quotes from Mary's reading material, divides opinion into three main, though not always distinct, categories- the attack on and rejection of religion, the defence of religion by apologists- often the same supportive writers quoted in the last chapter, and the positions of compromise.

Those who attacked religion, and specifically Christianity, tended to ridicule it as being for the needy and childish, setting science on the side of reason and at a higher level of proof and intellect, thus rendering religion outdated. Textual criticism of the Bible became part of the weaponry against religion. Virtue and civilised behaviour, it was suggested, were possible without religion and, in the absence of proof of a world to come, the aim should be to enjoy this world as much as possible. Some of the 'attacks' and critical questionings of the Bible were internal to the Church, notably from Bishop Colenso and the writers of essays and reviews who were attempting some accommodation with the new critics.

Apologists on the other hand, put faith above reason, often appealing to an intuitive experience of God, and also to an enhanced view of Him which they believed science actually presented. They advocated a more holistic approach, suggesting that scientists should not overstep their discipline, criticising the narrow outlook of many of them and condemning the destructive tendencies of sceptics, especially as regards the denial of immortality; also their arrogance, aggressive attitudes and lack of respect for such sacred texts as the Bible. They frequently took the view that there was little or no inherent conflict between religion and science. They sometimes asserted, rather than tried to prove, the glory of God and also quoted the numbers of scientists who remained Christian.

'Compromisers' is a slippery term but is here used to include those emphasising the need to extend love and tolerance to their 'opponents' (although this did not necessarily imply that they were ready to substantially compromise their views) or even happy to apply 'modifications' to their belief systems. It was felt, not infrequently, that clerics were trying too hard to accommodate themselves to the new dogmas. Many, most often from a position of Christian bias, were happy to trust to time for the evolution of knowledge, understanding and wisdom.

Here are a sample of opinions relevant to the three categories, drawn from Mary's reading (an author with broad or ambiguous views may appear in more than one section):

Views sceptical of religion/Christianity or the Bible

The superiority of science was often taken for granted by even such Christian writers as Hugh Miller, Scottish Geologist, who declared:

"*I trust, however, I may say I did first study and believe my Bible. But such is the structure of the human mind, that, save when blinded by passion or warped by prejudice, it must yield an involuntary consent to the force of evidence.*" (Miller, An Autobiography, 1856) p.442. (1870). (3/6.3.1856)

It was often felt that the theology that had hitherto prevailed was unsuited to the modern age and a threat to the freedoms now emerging. Mary read increasingly bold declarations:

"*It is now obvious that the theology of former ages cannot be permanently maintained*" (Somerset, Christian Theology and Modern Scepticism, 1872) p.8. (9/12.4.1872)

And some years later she perused *The Scientific Obstacles to Christian Belief* where it was stated:

"Christianity is entangled with such legacies of unreason from the past that the intractable knot admits of no easy solution, but must be violently cut." (Curteis, *The Scientific Obstacles to Christian Belief*, 1885) p.3. (15/5.7.1889)

Sometimes the Scriptures and the credulity of believers were ridiculed. Note Eliza Lynn, giving expression to this contempt in *The Autobiography of Christopher Kirkland*:

"The one wonder of his intercourse with me was that there should have ever been the time when I had believed in the creation of the world in six days, in the Incarnation, the Atonement, the Miracles, and the Devil; or that I should have hesitated as to my choice when I came to the age of reason" (Lynn, *The Autobiography of Christopher Kirkland*, 1885) vol 3, pp.255-256. (14/13.3.1886)

Sometimes religion was presented as unmanly:

"These tender souls are to virile thinkers what children are to men;" (Lynn, *The Autobiography of Christopher Kirkland*, 1885). vol 3. p.185. (14/13.3.1886)

And one way of putting religion down was to describe it as a 'natural' psychological need/process as opposed to a reality:

"From my present point of view, theology is regarded as a natural product of the operations of the human mind, under the conditions of its existence, just as any other branch of science, etc." (Huxley, *Essays upon Some Controverted Questions*, 1892) p.132. (16/25.8.1892)

Gospel history was denigrated and Renan, in his highly controversial *Life of Jesus*, opined:

> "*None of the miracles with which the old histories are filled took place under scientific conditions. Observation, which has not once been falsified, teaches us that miracles never happen but in times and countries in which they are believed, and before persons disposed to believe them.*" (Renan, *Life of Jesus*) Book 1, p.35. (London, Mathieson, 1890). (13/27.4.1884)

Genesis, in particular, was called into question, especially in view of the work of Charles Darwin which often generated an assumption, not necessarily made by Darwin himself, that God and evolution were incompatible. It was suggested that, with the expansion of science, god was receding, and a belief in evolution was taking its place:

> "*The more I think on the subject, the less I can see proof of design.*" (Darwin, *Life and letters of Charles Darwin*, 1888) vol 1, p.283. (1887). (14/31.5.1888)

> "*Everything points to a slow natural evolution.*" (Huxley, *Essays upon Some Controverted Questions*, 1892) p.46. (16/25.8.1892)

Religion, was sometimes described as one of the illusions of life - ironic, considering the Christian view that the world is itself illusory. Christopher Kirkland describes how:

> "To the individual, life is too often like a huge cynical joke where he is led by false hopes, mocked by illusive pleasures, pursued by phantom fears, and where he loses the joy of his desire so soon as he gains possession." (Lynn, *The Autobiography of Christopher Kirkland*, 1885) vol 3, p.182. (14/13.3.1886)

The position of the priest also is questioned in a fashionable novel:

> "To consecrate one's entire body and soul to a vast invisible that never speaks, that never answers, that gives no sign of either refusal or acquiescence to the most passionate prayers, to resign a thousand actual joys for the far-off dream of heaven" (Corelli, *Wormwood: A Drama of Paris*, 1890) vol 1, pp. 151-152. (15/4.2.1891)

Contrary to one of the central tenets of Christianity, the pleasures of this world might be considered a reasonable alternative to heaven:

> "Why should we forego the present, which is our own, for a future by which we shall not profit nor where we shall be found?" (Lynn, *The Autobiography of Christopher Kirkland*, 1885) vol 3, p.186. (14/13.3.1886)

Virtue and morality, it was suggested could exist independent of religion:

> "Nearly all the best Christians I know do not call themselves by that name." (Oliphant, *Altiora Peto*, 1883) vol 2, p.62. (13/27.11.1883)

> "Again, the sweet and patient moralities of Christianity are not special to Christians." (Lynn, *The Autobiography of Christopher Kirkland*, 1885) vol 3, p.156. (14/13.3.1886)

The blame for conflict was often placed squarely on religion, even sometimes by those who were advocates of religion:

> "Most of the sceptics of the present day are driven to their opinions by their consciences, which revolt against the current hypocrisy and glaring inconsistencies that characterise the profession of the popular theology." (Oliphant, *Piccadilly*, 1875) p.253. (1870). (13/29.3.1884)

Assertions of God and the Power of Christianity/Apologetics

The questionings about God, Christianity and the Bible were frequently seen by Christians as evil and dangerous to countenance, and they were often driven into a defensive position. Some of the quotations below are little more than expressions of disapproval or distress; others contain some reasoned argument:

"For Atheism separates truth from goodness, and Scepticism destroys truth altogether; both of which are monstrosities, from which we should revolt as from a real madness." (Arnold; Stanley, *The Life and Correspondence of Thomas Arnold*, 1846, p.382. (1844). (1/3.12.1847)

"The writings of infidels must, be read with caution and fear. There are cold, intellectual, speculative, malignant foes to Christianity." (Cecil, *The life and Remains of the Rev. Richard Cecil*, 1854) p.267. (London: Printed for Seeley, 1816). (3/28.9.1856)

"Herein lies the vast fallacy of the French skeptic. The worship of the merely Supernatural must, as science progresses, legitimately end in Atheism. Yes, all science removes the Cause of causes farther and farther back from human ken, so that the baffled intellect is compelled to confess at last we can not find it." (Robertson, *Sermons*, 1st Series, 1855 - 13 The Barbarian) (Robertson, *Sermons Preached at Brighton, by the late Rev. Frederick Robertson*, New York: Harper, 1905) p.157. (1860 onwards)

"The Essays in this volume are intended to offer aid to those whose faith may have been shaken by recent assaults." (Thomson, *Aids to Faith*, 1861) p.iii. (6/27.7.1862)

"We are told, indeed, that "the inevitable progress of research must, within a longer or shorter period, unravel all that *seems most marvellous."* (Thomson, *Aids to Faith*, 1861) p.14. (6/27.7.1862)

"In the last year of his personal administration of the diocese, writing to one, whose name subsequently became conspicuous in connexion with rationalistic doctrine, he said:- 'The question whether the Mosaic account of the creation can be reconciled with the discoveries of geology, is not a fit subject for discussion in the pulpit before a mixed congregation.'" (Blomfield, *A Memoir of Charles James Blomfield*, 1863) vol 2, p.174. (6/29.10.1863)

"If you could prove our Christian faith a fable, we could not live:- we could bear this life no more!" (Boyd, *The Graver Thoughts of a Country Parson*. 2nd Series, 1865) p.20. (Boston, Ticknor and Fields, 1865). (7/26.3.1865)

"Agnosticism!- that's what this 'search for truth' ends in nowadays" (Deland, *John Ward, Preacher*, 1889) p.427. (Boston: Houghton, Mifflin, 1888). (15/31.5.1889)

"For out of this that we call Atheism come so many other isms and falsities, each falsity with its misery at its heels!" (Carlyle, *Past and Present*, 1891). p.184. (1870). (15/20.12.1891)

"The attempts at founding a morality outside of religion are like what children do, when, wishing to transplant a plant to which they have taken a fancy, they tear off the root, which they do not like and which seems superfluous, and without the root stick the plant into the ground. Without a religious foundation, there can be no real, sincere morality, just as without a root there can be no real plant." (Tolstoy, *Walk in the Light While Ye Have Light*, 1905) pp. 541-542. (earlier edition not found) (15/16.1.1892)

The threat to immortality was of particular concern:

> "Mankind will bear a great deal, but it will not long bear the denial of a God of love, the attempt to thieve away the hope of being perfect and our divine faith in immortality." (Brooke, *Christ in Modern Life*, 1872) p.28. (12/6.11.1880)

> "We have a right to immortality which there are no reasonable grounds for disputing" (Momerie, *Preaching and Hearing*, 1888) p.287. (1890). (15/20.10.1889)

Some saw the more aggressive sceptics as arrogant or bullying:

> "We are persuaded by experience as well as certified by the word of God, that, as with the truly religious man, every fresh accession of knowledge, of what kind soever, teaches a lesson of humility, and adds to the materials of piety and thankfulness, so with the unbeliever and the profane- each step which is taken in the paths of science is one step further from God, inasmuch as it ministers to pride and self-sufficiency, and exalts understanding above conscience and the testimony of the

Spirit" (Bickersteth, *The Works of Rev E. Bickersteth, 1832*) p.147. (*A Scripture Help*, London, s.n., 1852). (16.6.1837)

"Scientific knowledge, even in the most modest persons, has mingled with it a something which partakes of insolence. Absolute, peremptory facts are bullies, and those who keep company with them are apt to get a bullying habit of mind;- not of manners, perhaps; they may be soft and smooth, but the smile they carry has a quiet assertion in it," (Holmes, *The Autocrat of the Breakfast Table*, 1883) p.46. (13/23.9.1883)

"But scientific certainty has no spring in it, no courtesy, no possibility of yielding. All this must react on the minds which handle these forms of truth." (Holmes, *The Autocrat of the Breakfast Table*, 1883) p.47. (13/23.9.1883)

There was a lack of respect for sacred things; textual criticism was especially disliked:

"The Bible scorns to be treated scientifically." (Cecil; Pratt, *The life and Remains of the Rev. Richard Cecil*, 1854) p.316 (London: Printed for Seeley, 1816). (3/28.9.1856)

Scepticism could be seen as unreasonable or a form of tunnel vision. Science should be kept within its own limited sphere and should not try to 'swallow up' religion:

"Only by a few is science studied now in the sublime and reverent spirit of old days. A vulgar demand for utility has taken the place of that lowly prostration with which the world listened to the discoveries of truth." (Robertson, Sermons, 2nd Series, 1855- 1 The Star in the East) (Robertson, Sermons Preached at Brighton, by the late Rev. Frederick W. Robertson, New York: Harper, 1905) p.253. (1860 onwards)

"It appears to me, however, that great mistakes are made in the expectations entertained with respect to what science can do. The scientific mode of viewing things is simply human; it is not God's way. Creation is one thing, - dissection is another." (Robertson; Brooke, Life and letters of Frederick W. Robertson, 1865) vol 2, p.46. (7/19.11.1865)

"Science comes and gives us an explanation which kills the livingness in the wind and the joy in the sea." (Brooke, Sermons Preached in St. James's Chapel, 1871) p.120. (9/11.5.1873)

"It is this forgetfulness which tends to make scientific men what they sometimes are, monsters of abnormal intellectual development." (Brooke, Sermons Preached in St. James's Chapel, 1871) p.122. (9/18.7.1873)

"This is why men merely scientific fail to see the beauty and truth of Christianity. They bring to the examination of the highest phenomena only the same kind of eye which serves them in the lower. They see nothing, and then employ the authority of their acquired eminence in "science" to persuade men there is nothing to see!" (Philpot, *A Pocket of Pebbles*, 1877) no.77. (11/3.3.1878)

"The history of science is the history of exhausted errors." (Brooke, *Christ in Modern Life*, 1880) p.301. (New York: Appleton, 1877). (12/6.11.1880)

"Duncan avoided one great danger connected with such physical studies- the narrowing, purely intellectual tendencies they are apt to engender. He wisely co-ordinated them with wider social and religious subjects possessing humanitarian relations." (Jolly, *The life of John Duncan*, 1883) p.497. (14/14.6.1888)

"Each science, I repeat, is supreme within its own domain; but it has no sovereign authority beyond it." (Westcott, *The Gospel of Life*, 1892) p.90. (16/28.6.1893)

Many more felt there was no conflict between science and religion or that they were complementary:

"Nor, be it remarked, is there positive atheism involved in the belief. God might as certainly have originated the species by a law of development;- the existence of a First Great Cause is as perfectly compatible with the first scheme as with the other." (Miller, *Foot-prints of the Creator*, 1850). p.13 (1849). (2/15.5.1852)

"What we miss in science is supplied by religion. Thus

we possess *Two revelations, which confirm and establish each other: ... The contradictions, however, are but in appearance, and vanish before the eye of inquiry. 'The two Revelations' are perfectly distinct, and when viewed together, should be considered with a clear perception and recognition of the individual purpose of each."* (Fullom, *The Marvels of Science and Their Testimony to Holy Writ*, 1854) p.124. (1853). (3/16.2.1855)

"Nor let it be forgotten how disastrous has ever been the influence of the opinion that theologians teach one thing, and men of science another." (Hitchcock, *The Religion of Geology and Its Connected Sciences*, 1856) p.69. (Boston: Phillips, Sampson, 1857). (3/29.9.1856)

"Why, then, should it not be taught to children, that they may not be liable to distrust the whole Bible, when they come to the study of geology? Soon shall the horizon, where geology and revelation meet, be cleared of every cloud, and present only an unbroken and magnificent circle of truth." (Hitchcock, *The Religion of Geology and Its Connected Sciences*, 1856) p.70. (Boston: Phillips, Sampson,1857). (3/29.9. 1856)

"It has been said that the inferences of the geologist militate against those of the theologian. Nay, not those of our higher geologists and higher theologians." (Miller, *The Testimony of the Rocks*, 1858) p.265. (1857). (4/14.1.1858)

"Men will accept the assertion, easily made and difficult to be refuted, yet, like every such assertion, demanding care and

watchfulness in its acceptance, that science contradicts the Bible; when perhaps it is their ignorance of science which makes the statement formidable, and when sometimes the most truly scientific man has also been the most believing." (Vaughan, Lessons of life and Godliness, 1862) p.350. (*Lessons of Life and Godliness and Words from the Gospels*, 1891). (6/9.11.1862)

"Of this I am quite sure, that where the study of God's works is combined with a sure faith in His Word, the former can in no respect impair our spiritual possession of the life that now is, or deprive us of the enjoyment of one jot or tittle of those glorious promises which have assured to us a blessed immortality." (Jenyns, *Memoir of the Rev. John Stevens Henslow*, 1862) p.154. (6/26.7.1863)

"Fully satisfied that religion and science cannot in reality be at variance. (scientist should pursue his observations to the good of both)" (Lubbock, *Pre-historic Times*, 1865) p.viii. (8/12.3.1867)

"The preacher disappointed me. He was for dividing faith and reason, while I am for uniting them; true reason must ever support true faith, since they both come from God." (Hare, A., *Memorials of a Quiet Life*, 1873) p.132. (1872). (9/21.8.1873)

"Supposing Christianity had committed itself to any scientific statements or to any scientific method, it could never have been fitted to expand with the expansion of knowledge, to be a religion for a race which is continually advancing in scientific knowledge. ... It is no more in actual opposition to science than poetry is. ... But there are hundreds of things which are not and cannot be submitted to such a proof." (Brooke, *Christ in Modern Life:*, 1880) p.24. (New York: Appleton, 1877). (12/6.11.1880)

"He considers that the theory of Evolution is quite compatible with the belief in a God; but that you must remember that different persons have different definitions of what they mean by God." (Darwin, *Life and letters of Charles Darwin*, 1888) vol 1, p.307. (14/31.5.1888)

"An assurance is rapidly dawning upon us all that there is no essential contradiction between science and Christianity." (Curteis, *The Scientific Obstacles to Christian Belief*, 1885) p.173. (15/5.7.1889)

"Between true science and true religion there never has been, never will be, never can be, any conflict whatever. ... And because these false antagonisms have been infinitely dangerous to faith over Darwin's grave, let us once more assure the students of science that for us the spirit of mediaeval ecclesiasticism is dead." (Farrar, *Social and Present Day Questions*, 1892) p.308. (15/22.5.1892)

"But while this is so, there can be no opposition between Reason and Faith. Most significant that the popular antithesis of reason and faith finds no place in Scripture. In Scripture the opposite to faith is Sight." (Westcott, *The Gospel of Life*, 1892) p.xx. (16/28.6.1893)

Science was not necessarily the enemy of religion but could enhance our perception of the greatness of God:

> "All God's works shall in everything bring glory to his name, and evidence and illustration to the truth and fullness of his revealed word." (Bickersteth, *The Works of Rev E. Bickersteth, 1832*) p.120. (*A Scripture Help*, London, s.n., 1852). (16.6.1837)

> "We shall endeavour to show that the bearings of all science, when rightly understood, are eminently favourable to religion, both in this world and the next." (Hitchcock, *The Religion of Geology*, 1856) p.27. (Boston: Phillips, Sampson,1857). (3/29.9.1856)

> "Science has in fact, in this case, become a revelation. ... Let us rather hail Science as a handmaid to religion." (Farrar, Adam, *Science in Theology*, 1859) p.84. (5/24.3.1861)

> "Yet, they who can look back a few years will remember how the same pulpits, then rebuking and maligning the conclusions at which geologists had arrived, are now content to accept them as evidence of a Wisdom, Power, and Goodness, beyond any that former ignorance could ascribe to the works of that First Great cause, which spake the word, and they were made;

> commanded, and they were created." (Jenyns, *Memoir of the Rev. John Stevens Henslow*, 1862) p.218. (6/ 26.7.1863)

> "All is in order and harmony, and for long ages men believed, naturally enough, that their habitation was the central and only object of God's care. The whole of the earth's history may be but as a day in the history of the universe, ... Every day's history is the key and the clue to the history of ages long since past." (Ansted, *The Great Stone Book of Nature*, 1863) p.11. (6/13.8.1863)

> "The study of physical science elevates our notion of the Deity and renders us conscious of an invisible intelligence and power far surpassing the sublimest visions which the Hebrew prophets ever believed." (Somerset, *Christian Theology and Modern Scepticism*, 1872) p.171. (9/12.4.1872)

Evolution itself could be a brilliant work of God:

> "The true wisdom is to see in all the steps of this earth's progress the guiding hand of God, and to believe that He will not leave to itself the world which for His own pleasure He has created." (Clodd, *The Childhood of the World*, 1876) p.55. (11/13.2.1877)

> "But if He be with mankind as He is with Himself, present through and in the ages as their heart and brain, then He is the source whence evolution flows. And because He is perfect, therefore the race evolves towards perfection, and evolution towards

perfection is progress." (Brooke, *Christ in Modern Life*, 1880) p.308. (New York: Appleton, 1877). (12/6.11.1880)

"For the goal of Evolution is Jesus Christ. The Christian life is the only life that will never be completed." (Drummond, *Natural Law in the Spiritual World*, 1883) p.314. (New York: Pott, 1884). (13/13.7.1884)

"For this favourite theory is supposed, in some quarters, to stand in flagrant contradiction to the idea of a Divine creation. But since the hypothesis of Evolution is nothing else than an attempt to explain how the heavens and the earth were created, leaving the statement quite untouched that they were created. .... The one simply takes up the story where the other leaves it off." (Curteis, *The Scientific Obstacles to Christian Belief*, 1885) pp.56/57. (15/5.7.1889)

"What harm can come to religion, even if it be demonstrated, not only that God is so wise that He can make all things, but that He is so much wiser even than that, that He can make all things make themselves." (Hetherington, Burton, *Paul Nugent-Materialist*, 1891) p.273. (15/9.3.1891)

"God's way of making worlds is to make them make themselves." (Drummond, *The City Without a Church*, 1893) p.15. (In 'The Programme of Christianity- An Address'). (16/9.4.1893)

And often the assertion of God's omnipotence, and the

dependence of the world upon Him, was made without specific arguments:

> "What is a natural law without the presence and energizing power of the lawgiver? Take away God from the universe, or let him cease to act mentally upon it, and every movement would as instantly and certainly cease, as would every movement of the human frame, were the mind to be withdrawn, or cease to will." (Hitchcock, *The Religion of Geology and Its Connected Sciences*, 1856) p.293. (Boston: Phillips, Sampson,1857). (3/29.9.1856)

> "Study nature- not scientifically- that would take eternity, to do it so as to reap much moral good from it. Superficial physical science is the devil's spade, with which he loosens the roots of the trees prepared for the burning! Do not study matter for its own sake, but as the countenance of God" (Kingsley; Kingsley, *Charles Kingsley: His Letters and Memories of His Life*, 1877) vol 1, p.88. (11/1.4.1877)

> "Science has a God; and he who believes in this, in spite of all protest, possesses a theology." (Drummond, *Natural Law in the Spiritual World*, 1883) p.162. (New York: Pott, 1884). (13/13.7.1884)

> "Here science leaves us, but only to conclude, from other grounds, that there is a First Cause to which all others are secondary and ministrative, a primitive almighty will, of which these laws are merely the mandates." (Chambers; Ireland,

Vestiges of the Natural History of Creation, 1884) p.28. (London: Routledge, 1887). (13/10.2.1885)

Some, like Frederick Robertson, appealed to the special intuitive, experiential knowledge and faith possessed by devoted Christians:

> "Christ told all, but by the intuitions of the soul, not by science." (Robertson; Brooke, *Life and letters of Frederick W. Robertson*, 1865) vol 2, p.48. (7/19.11.1865)

Mary, a devotee of his preaching, clearly believed in a non-rational approach to faith based on religious experience, intuition and a personal relationship with Christ. In response to reading correspondence, following a published letter of Gladstone which argued passionately against the declaration of Papal infallibility by the Vatican Council, she advocated restraint in argument , ... *Always remembering that beyond the bounds of controversy there are mysteries of life and death insoluble & often to be felt in the hidden recesses of the heart, soul, or spirit of man, in communion and harmony with the Supreme Spirit of life & death which pervades the Universe - the prayer of life, Thy Will be done; of death, 'Father, into thy hands I commend my spirit.'* (It is not clear if this is a quotation.) (10/15.11.1874)

The theme is echoed in the following extracts:

> "The Holy Spirit thus gives Christians an illumination far beyond mere head-knowledge." (Bickersteth, *The Works of*

Rev E. Bickersteth, 1832) p.42. (*A Scripture Help*, London, s.n.,1852). (16.6.1837)

"The racking misery of a mind striving to satisfy itself by its own reasoning, in questions which faith alone can answer" (Sewell, *The Experience of Life*, 1853) p.59. (2/19.10.1853)

"There is a power in the soul, quite separate from the intellect, which sweeps away or recognizes the marvellous, by which God is felt. Faith stands serenely far above the reach of the atheism of science intellect does not even pretend to judge or recognize." (Robertson, *Sermons*, 1st Series, 1855-13 *The Barbarian*) (Robertson, *Sermons Preached at Brighton, by the late Rev. Frederick W. Robertson*, New York: Harper, 1905), p.157. (1860 onwards)

"The whole world is one grand demonstration of life to encourage us in the sure conviction of life eternal" (Jenyns, *Memoir of the Rev. John Stevens Henslow*, 1862) p.257. (6/26.7.1863)

"So in the higher life of man, there are strange instincts. There are impressions we cannot account for; there are moments when we seem to stand out beyond ourselves." (Davies, *Orthodox London*, 1876). pp.30-31. (1874). (13/30.11.1884)

Some of the apologists were prone to cite the number of scientists who remained Christian, in illustration of their cause:

"That God has been recognised and worshipped by men of infinitely higher genius, of infinitely greater eminence, than any atheist or agnostic living or dead." (Momerie, Preaching and Hearing, 1888) p.116. (1890). (15/20.10.1889)

"He has been called an infidel and atheist so often that there is a wide-spread belief to this effect, but nothing could be further from the truth. Darwin was a firm believer in a First Cause. He was in theory an agnostic, in practice an orthodox Christian of the broadest type." (Holder, Charles Darwin, 1891) p.148. (1892). (15/11.10.1891)

"Many an earnest believer in the Lord Jesus Christ bent with sorrowing heart over Darwin's grave." (Farrar, Social and Present Day Questions, 1892) p.303. (15/22.5.1892)

Compromisers

Compromise was often regarded as necessary. There were many who felt that theology should yield to the discoveries of science and many who favoured the restraint of science in order to avoid any clashes with time-honoured theological beliefs:

"My sincere desire in the composition of the book was to give the true view of the history of nature, with as little disturbance as possible to existing beliefs, whether philosophical or religious." (Chambers, Ireland, Vestiges of the Natural

History of Creation, 1884) p.285. (London: Routledge, 1887). (13/10.2.1885)

Some suggested the modification of theology to meet science halfway or postulated different versions of God:

> "*The science of the geologist seems destined to exert a marked influence on that of the natural theologian.*" (Miller, *The Testimony of the Rocks*, 1858) p.192. (1857). (4/14.1.1858)

> "*The clergy have often done great damage to the truth. They have sought more to fit in what has been proposed as truth to them, to a system of theology given them in the Divinity hall, than to see it in the light of God himself.*" (Macleod, *Memoir of Norman Macleod*, 1876) vol 2, p.315. (10/15.4.1876)

> "*Geology at first seems inconsistent with the authority of the Mosaic record. A storm of unreasoning indignation rises against its teachers. In time, its truths, being found quite irresistible, are admitted, and mankind continue to regard the Scriptures with the same respect as before. So also with several other sciences.*" (Chambers; Ireland, *Vestiges of the Natural History of Creation*, 1884) p.285. (London: Routledge, 1887). (13/10.2.1885)

But a fairly common Christian reaction to the incoming flood of scepticism and textual criticism was simply to invoke Christian love and tolerance:

"Cultivate a spirit of tender love towards all from whom you differ." (Bickersteth, *The Works of Rev E. Bickersteth, 1832*) p.126. (*A Scripture Help*, London, s.n., 1852). (16.6.1837)

"They hope that these Essays may be, to those whose attention they can secure, incentives to further thought and reading. They have avoided rather than sought direct controversy. They have excluded personality; they have not spoken with undue harshness of the views they have been forced to oppose." (Thomson, *Aids to Faith*, 1861) p.iii. (5/27.7.1862)

"Men need to be told now, as much as they ever did, that controversy, to be Christian, must be conducted in a Christian spirit of forbearing love" (Davidson; Benham. *Life of Archibald Campbell Tait*, 1891) vol 1, p.477. (15/28.6.1891)

"All sciences end in theology. Therefore it is with joy and the kindling hope of reaching higher truths about the Divine that we listen to all that men of science tell us." (Brooke, *The Fight of Faith*, 1879) p.274. (King 1877). (12/9.11.1879)

Some of the more mature and self-assured religionists and some sitting on the fence saw no hurry to prove anything: not everything needed to be known now:

"What new and astonishing avenues of knowledge does this subject show us will probably open upon the soul in eternity" (Hitchcock, *The Religion of Geology and Its Connected*

Sciences, 1856) p.442. (Boston: Phillips, Sampson,1857). (3/ 29.9.1856)

"On this principle there may, of course, be portions of the prophetic pre-Adamic past of as doubtful interpretation at the present time, from the imperfect development of historic events. The science necessary to the interpretation of the one may be as certainly still to discover as the events necessary to the interpretation of the other may be still to take place." (Miller, The Testimony of the Rocks, 1858) p.174. (1857). (4/ 14.1.1858)

"There is a time coming, and now not very distant, when the vagaries of the anti-geologists will be as obsolete as those of the geographers of Salamanca, ... It will then be seen by all what a noble vestibule the old geologic ages form to that human period in which moral responsibility first began on earth, and a creature destined to immortality anticipated an eternal hereafter. There is always much of the mean and the little in the worlds which man creates for himself, and in the history which he gives them." (Miller, The Testimony of the Rocks, 1858) pp.420-421. (1857). (4/14.1.1858)

"For all is the work of one Almighty Power, and has been elaborated from the beginning as part of one vast, comprehensive, and infinitely wise scheme, in which apparent interruptions and interpolations have been foreseen, and are but parts of the full and complete development of an original plan. We may never in this life succeed in discovering the whole plan, for it is not likely that finite powers can grasp the Infinite design. But each endeavour that is made, humbly and honestly, will be productive of good." (Ansted, *The Great Stone Book of Nature*, 1863) p.334. (6/13.8.1863)

"Dr. Beattie holds that our Creator has permitted us to know just a very little; and the sagacious Dr. Paley affirms that what we do not know, need not disturb our belief in what we do know." (Smiles, *Robert Dick*, 1878) p.188. (4/30.12 1878)

"To reconcile this to the recognised character of the Deity, it is necessary to suppose that the present system is but part of a whole, a stage in a Great Progress, and that the Redress is in reserve." (Chambers, Ireland, *Vestiges of the Natural History of Creation*, 1884) p.282. (London: Routledge, 1887). (3/10.2.1885)

"May it not be that the souls which are meant to flower most gloriously towards God have to grope about a long time in doubt and uncertainty?" (Curteis, *The Scientific Obstacles to Christian Belief*, 1885) p.4. fn. (quoting Schleiermacher, *Rede über Religion*, p.150). (5/5.7.1889)

"But none of it has a scientific value, a certitude arising from proof and experience. And indeed it cannot have this, for it professes to be an anticipation of a state of things not yet actually experienced." (Arnold, *Literature and Dogma*, 1889). p.104. (Edinburgh: Nelson, 1873). (15/19.3.1890)

A number of writers felt that the controversies could have positive results:

> "SOME are disposed to condemn at once all controversial studies, as prejudicial and unprofitable; but it has pleased God to turn even opposition to his truth to good, and make it instrumental to the advancement of that which it was intended to overthrow." (Bickersteth, *The Works of Rev E. Bickersteth*, 1832) p.92. (*A Scripture Help*, London, s.n., 1852). (16/6/1837)

> "Let us remark how God makes good come at last out of the painful differences of good men." (Boyd, *The Graver Thoughts of a Country Parson*, 2nd series, 1865) p.89. (Boston, Ticknor, 1865). (6/2.8.1863)

> "For the impulse of science, justified by the long wrestle of centuries, is becoming itself religious,- and there is a new awe rising on the brow of Knowledge." (Ward, *The History of David Grieve*, 1892) p.481. (15/2.4.1892)

Norman Macleod, Scottish clergyman and author, demonstrated the blessed ability, rare in these matters, to respond with proportion:

> "Some of the most portentous attacks on the faith, provoked his sense of humour more than his alarm." (Macleod, *Memoir of Norman Macleod*, 1876) vol 2, p.234. (10/15.4.1876)

But Mary, herself, could make the last observation here:

> *Finished Jewish Church book & was charmed with it-* There is a note at the end referring to Colenso's work which had not appeared till after this was written- ending with the observation that religion must gain not lose from criticism in a right spirit.

5

The Gardens

"Sometimes he dug in his garden; again, he read or wrote. He had but one word for both these kinds of toil; he called them gardening. 'The mind is a garden,' said he."
(Hugo, *Les Misérables*, 1862) vol 1, p.17. (New York: Crowell, 1887) (6/28.7.1862)

They smell of Uffington, that is enough for me.
Mary's Diaries (20.4.1837)

Clutching some bedraggled violets, sent from her house in the country and misrouted on their way to London, the fifteen-year-old Mary Pegus, with the above words, expressed her profound rootedness in home and garden. This affirmation is remarkable for its occurrence so soon after the accidental drowning of Elizabeth, her loved younger sister and companion, in the canal at Uffington; her love of the place survived even the death of her sister. But it is Monsieur Myriel, Bishop of Digne, a character at the beginning of Victor Hugo's *Les Misérables*, read by Mary in the summer and autumn of 1862, who gives us a lead into our subject; the mind of Mary, Marchioness of Huntly, was also a garden, and she walked and worked all through her life in both her mental and material gardens.

A large country home with its garden, and often its surrounding estate or countryside, could form an almost complete world, especially for a child. The Uffington estate in Lincolnshire, the home at this time of the Earls of Lindsey, and Mary's childhood home, was in Uffington, a village in the valley of the River Welland, two miles from Stamford; its parish church was dedicated to St Michael & All Angels. The Orton estate in Huntingdonshire, to the south-west of Peterborough, then a residence of the Marquises of Huntly, was Mary's marital home. This estate was in Orton Longueville, a parish on a bank of the River Nene; its church was Holy Trinity. The massive Aboyne estate, Deeside, Aberdeenshire, where Mary and her family often stayed, was the first residence of the Marquises of Huntly, although the Orton estate was generally used as the main home.

Upper- and upper-middle class girls left home on occasion to visit cities, homes of relatives, seaside resorts and foreign parts, but Mary never forgot her gardens even for a moment. On one occasion she *fell asleep & dreamt of Uffington* (9.7.1835), and on another, ***bought some beautiful flowers & thought myself at Uffington.*** (30.5.1840). Whatever the attractions of the outside world, they were always rivalled by the lure of home. Mary referred in her late teens to ***agreeable & intellectual society on one hand & the love of home on the other.*** (30.8.1841)

Characteristic of this period is the coexistence of large country gardens and parks with women who increasingly roamed, cultivated and wrote about them, taking initiative in their management. The countryside around a mansion, containing areas of wilderness, formed, not only a context for the gardens, but also a shared space between neighbours. Within this space were country towns, flower shows, local dances and various other diversionary spaces and events, and these areas also encompassed the political, judicial and administrative activities of the larger country house owners. Mary, demonstrating her appreciation of the rural way of life, wrote, ***To see the country people enjoying their walk on a fine Sunday always gives me a happy feeling.*** (28.4.1839)

Once she reported:

> *There was a long argument upon the characteristic superiority versus inferiority of country gentlemen. It is needless to say in defence of which opinion I enlisted my best oratorical power.* (3.9.1843)

She always tended to prefer the outside world of the garden, not only because of a love of nature, but also because the indoor atmosphere was often uncongenial. She once wrote at age fifteen:

> *I went down into the drawing room & stayed there some time not speaking a word for a very good reason because every one was so much engulfed with their own concerns that they could not speak to me.* (18.7.1837)

Nature to Mary was a manifestation of the Creator, and virtually always held a positive value for her as it did for many Christian clerics and writers of the age. The 'dark side' of the natural world, storms, volcanoes etc. were regretted by her, but did not alter her basic outlook.

I ran out in the garden – and altho' it was very cold I found it quite a relief to be secure at least for a few minutes from any more poignant attacks than those of wind & rain, cried myself to sleep. (18.7.1837)

Mary also wrote, aged thirteen, of the **serenity and sunshine of the mind** (11.10.1835), and often discussed the tendency of weather, operating through the senses, to transform mood and perception. One day, she **cantered about & enjoyed myself much**, declaring *This is one of those calm soft & exhilarating days when nature seems to smile away all unpleasant feelings which may be warring within.* Character could be thus improved and she continued:

> *Since writing the above I have met with a passage in*

Sharon Farmer's Sacred History displaying the concordance of our feelings, with the beauties of Nature. Love, friendship, independence, are all in harmony with these beauties. Self-love, vanity, assurance are in dissonance with them. (28.12.1837)

Years later she described how she *started to peregrinate alone in no very happy spirits tho' the bright sun & soft airs were peculiarly calculated to drive away melancholy.* (13.3.1843). Air quality was felt conducive to a clear head and right thinking, as when she went to Kew: *I enjoyed the fresh air - a resolution to bear crosses more lightly & at any rate to be independent.* (8/4.7.1869). Some years later in Scotland, she *tried to take heart again mid all the beautiful surroundings of nature.* (11/27.9.1877)

The enjoyment of Nature and the practice of botany were activities still much recommended for children and young ladies and Mary developed a passion for botany which led to numerous countryside excursions in search of wild plants; also a project of classification which produced, after many years, a substantial herbarium. But her studies in natural history and in botanical classification, whilst representing a scientific approach, did not lead her anywhere close to a sense of conflict between science and religion; indeed her scientific knowledge of geology and plants helped make her accommodating to both, in common with many of her favourite authors and preachers and she continued to praise God for the beauty and abundance of Nature.

Reverence for 'Nature' was widespread through the century and the works she read often reflected her sentiments.

> "He saw that this earth and skies are God's garment- the garment by which we see God. (Kingsley, *Twenty-five Village Sermons*, 1854) p.6. (1857). (3/14.1.1856)

> "The Poet, nor less his sister, came at length to feel, what philosophers find so hard to believe, - that The Being whom he had long known as near him in the solitudes of nature, as close to the beatings of his own heart, was He who had so loved him as to die for him." (Wordsworth, D., *Recollections of a tour made in Scotland*, 1874) p.xl. (10/27.2.1875)

> "The older I get I find more and more teaching from God's revelation in nature." (Macleod, *Memoir of Norman Macleod*, 1876) vol 1, p.383. (New York: Worthington). (10/15.4.1876)

> He who is taught to see and delight in the colour of a primrose has something henceforth in him which will go far to keep him from cruelty to his wife." (Brooke, *Christ in Modern Life*, 1880) p.267. (New York: Appleton, 1877). (12/16.11.1880)

Ironically Mary has been held responsible by botanical historians, Sheail and Wells, for possibly contributing to the depletion of stocks of wildflowers in the Cambridgeshire area. This was because she habitually uprooted wild plants in order to replant them in her gardens. As she grew older, she came to be aware of the necessary limits to collecting. The plundering of nature for personal gratification or, on a larger scale, in the cause of urban and industrial development, rose high on her list of concerns, feeding into a devotion to conservation. In 1860, Mary referred to the depradations of *some rapacious fern-collector* and she was sensitive, especially later in her life, to any destruction of the countryside. (5/30.6.1860). This was expressed repeatedly: *The rage for flowers is now so great that evidently it is a lucrative trade.* (13/2.6.1884); *The piece of waste ground had all been eaten down by sheep. Alas there will soon be no place left for wild flowers.* (14/8.9.1885); *It was curious to see in that part of the wood which was not cut down two years ago the quantity of flowers that have appeared spontaneously having not been there before.* (15/10.7.1889); *After a careful search we failed to discover one plant of the Bee Orchis in its old haunts. Other plants have also disappeared & it is difficult to account for this.* (15/22.6.1892)

Mary was always anxious about the effects of building development: *Drove to Hampstead Heath so altered that I scarcely knew it again but there is still a great deal of ground not built upon and very beautiful it is Gorse & Broom in flower.* (15/25.5.1889)

She also showed the instincts of a conservationist in the running of the estates. Although avenues were common territory for family and public access, Strath's view prevailed in the creation of this space and, whilst he was planting large numbers of Wellingtonias, which were newly imported and fashionable, she was left pleading for the lives of old trees which were now obstructing progress: *Walked in the afternoon to see the line of road suggested for getting into the avenue from the house. I begged that the old Elm trees might be spared & the road kept on the right of them.* (4/13.12.1859); *saw Davie cutting down the oak on the lawn near the entrance, which I must say I regret though it is too late to save it. A Wellingtonia is to be planted in its place.* (7/7.11.1865). But she became protective of the Wellingtonias in their turn: *Walked with Mr Berkeley to see the Wellingtonias which Mr Phillips shot instead of the pheasants. Very disagreeable day.* (7/28.12.1865). The concern for trees continued: *Saw Hobbs men were cutting the trees and feared they were taking more than had been marked.* (12/9.1.1882); *fed rabbits and went with Harding to see gaps left by wood cutting which made me unhappy.* (12/14.1.1882)

The garden has sometimes been described as potentially fulfilling the function of 'intermediate space' and that notion is supported here in four senses:

1 The garden was materially intermediate between the house and the outside world. The grounds or some portion of them were traversed in journeys outwards and would be encountered, often with joy, by the residents, on their inward journeys, as familiar sights reappeared and new growth or change was detected. On her return from London to Uffington soon after her sister's death, Mary's emotions were heightened. She wrote, *What feelings were there that shot through me as I again came within sight of the old house & Church.* (13.5.1837). The following day she *passed Uffington Wood & could not resist the temptation of looking. Bluebells, cowslips, & orchises vied with each other in giving it the appearance of an immense bed of flowers.*(14.5.1837). Years later, on

returning to Orton, she *found the dear chicks all well & the place looking beautifully green with all the Spring blossoms.* (3/2.6.1855)

Visitors also moved from the outer world to the mansion via the drive or other approach and, more often than not, would be taken on a tour of the rest of the grounds, not only for fresh air, exercise and private discussion, but also to demonstrate the garden's assets. Imposed structures, such as railways and canals, furthermore, linked home and the outside world in a definitive way. Because these gardens were so spacious and wild on the periphery, they almost merged with the land exterior to the boundaries; plants could also provide a connection with faraway places.

2 The garden was a relaxed space where those of different ages, genders and classes could meet with reduced formality. It was not only a place of fresh air, healthy activity and home education, but also a site of family activities and togetherness. **We walked in the garden**, **We took a turn in the garden**, **Walked in the garden with,** or similar words, feature prominently in Mary's diaries, alongside the simple: **Walked in the garden** which suggests a stroll taken alone. In Mary's case, **we** and **I** alternated frequently as she ventured out in sociable or solitary mode and **walk** and **talk** were often juxtaposed, linking physical exercise with the exercising of thoughts and observations. Implicit was the suggestion that the garden would provide a congenial environment for social intercourse. The following narrative appears in Mary's childhood diary:

> *Walked with Lindsey and Elizabeth to the spring where we found Betts and Connolly. We followed them into the plantation at the bottom of the park and there we watched them ... . We then pursued our walk down the avenue and found Mama walking down the second, she joined us until we reached the house, when she & Lindsey went indoors and Papa and Mr. Thomson who had been walking down the farm walked us two round by the river to see the heifers. Sweep walked with us all the afternoon.* (25.1.1835)

The potential of a large garden such as Uffington can be no better illustrated than by Mary's ability here to find social reward with co-residents that even the highly resourceful Charlotte found frustrating, her abrasive father, depressed mother and two half-brothers, Lindsey who was mentally disabled and Bertie (not present on the aforegoing occasion) who was somewhat self-contained. Although sociable and affectionate by nature, Mary, in her youth, was selective in her friendships, warming uncritically to family members, friends, children and people in need, but disliking those she perceived as false or socially frivolous, treating them in her diary as a reference group to which she compared herself as an outsider. Note Mary and her husband together at Orton:

> *Strath took a little walk with me & we bid the garden good bye & the nursery of plants under the old oak tree which is the result of so many pleasant rambles during the last 6 weeks past.* (1/19.7.1846)

Also:

> Walked with S. in the garden & afterwards with Miss D & the children who with their Papa's help made a snow ball. We went out again in the afternoon & began building a snow house. (2/11.2.1853); Walked with S. to the Lady's well before luncheon & in the afternoon with him & the 5 elder chicks in the plantations on the west of the Castle towards Charleston. (3/23.9.1855); S. returned at 6. & walked up to the hayfield with Mary. (2/11.2.1853); The elder ones worked at their gardens & Douggy went round the wilderness with me. ... Long Walk cricket & bowls on the lawn where Gracie & Esmae joined us. (4/17.6.1857)

On occasion, an amble through the garden could become a preparation for a journey through the world, as when, much later in life, Nellie, one of Mary's daughters, was *accompanied by George Wickham, who told me in the evening that they had made up their minds to enter upon the walk of life together.* (13/7.12.1884)

The Long Walk, created at Orton, became a grand display of monumental trees destined to impress current neighbours and posterity, but was also the main approach and departure route for visitors, a meeting-place for all the family, a favourite venue for Mary to walk or ride and, occasionally, a shooting location. The lawns were the site of innumerable games of croquet, cricket and other sports, a place for picnics and a gentle environment for invalids such as Strath, in his final days, to take fresh air. The pond in the kitchen garden was used every winter for skating, and rabbit hutches and animal pens were constructed for the children's pets. (5/26.12.1860). Mary, never lacking in a sense of fun, nor in an appreciation of the familial, entered into the spirit of all these activities inasmuch as weariness from the stresses of bearing fourteen children would allow her. She skated on the pond with her children, enjoyed the family pets and accommodated herself to the pace and interests of children, husband, visitors and invalids (first Strath, later herself). For example: *Went out for half an hour before luncheon in the garden with dear S. the first time he has been out.* (4/31.12.1857); *Walked with dear S. as far as the old oak tree & back.* (4/20.2.1859); *Accompanied them* (her children) *in the garden chair to the farm & home by the Long Walk.* (4/1.5.1859)

3 The garden could be a space of empowerment for women between the restricted world of home and the public domain. This applies even to upper-class women who, whilst enjoying a substantial role in public and social life, had often been unwelcome in scientific and learned spheres and sometimes in the company of garden designers and innovators. The unambitious and conventional young lady and the aspirant to greater artistic and scientific achievement and personal advancement could use and experience the garden, often in different ways, and the interests of both were served. Usually, gardens were positive places for elite women, not only because they were likely to be spacious, beautiful and peaceful, but sometimes also because they were supplemented by a 'public' life both within and without their boundaries.

For well-connected women like Mary the public and private were closely intermingled. So the curiosity aroused by the finding of an unknown plant by Mary and Strath was translated speedily into an enquiry to the most eminent horticultural journalists of the day. *Found a pretty water plant probably a Cardamine which we brought home. Sent ... to the editors of the Gardener's Chronicle, to be named.* (4/21.5.1844). This relationship with figures in public life was, for Mary, like others of her rank, a simple everyday fact.

Such women were also privileged amongst their gardening peers in having substantial land, easy access to the gardens of other landowners, and relatives and friends with botanical or horticultural experience and knowledge, all of which placed them in a prestigious class-based arena in which they were able to contact many experts and make themselves and their activities known. Huntly reported that his mother's main correspondents were Rev. Charles Kingsley, Rev. M.J. Berkeley (a specialist in fungi), and Mr G H Marsh, a friend from her youth (knowledgeable about wild flowers and fossils), who was distantly connected with Bishop Davis of Peterborough and had taken holy orders. He had contributed much of Mary's collection from Central Europe. Rev. Wolley-Dod, a legend in garden history circles, was also mentioned:

> In the afternoon, to Edge, the pretty place belonging to Mr. Wooley Dodd. Unfortunately the owner was absent but we made a diligent survey of the beautiful ... & herbaceous garden & saw many most interesting plants cultivated with great success. It is famed as one of the finest if not the finest collection in England. (14/12.4.1886)

Another acquaintance was George Druce, an eminent local botanist and author of such botanical publications as *The Flora of Northamptonshire*, in which he referred to Mary's rockery as "one of the earliest of its kind in Europe." Another was Reverend Hugh Neville Dixon, a local gardener and amateur botanist who specialised in grasses; another the Rev. Samuel Reynolds Hole, rose specialist and author. All these men, most of them 'botanical clergymen,' were intermittent or constant friends and influences in Mary's life.

Some of Mary's relatives, the Layards from her mother's side of the family, shared their expertise with her and brought her plants from newly discovered lands, so that Mary was connected to an international world of plant discovery. Also, in the normal course of her social life, she conversed with a number of horticulturally minded landowners. She mentioned how Lord Fitzwilliam **walked to look at the Wellingtonias & inspected the curiousities in the way of fossils china &c.** Mary was clearly flattered by the attention, commenting that: *It is not often that any one shows so much interest in my rubbish.* (10/31.7.1876). Some years later, she accompanied Colonel Coates **over the garden & rockery** noting that *he was much interested in the conifers of which he has himself a collection.* (14/21.6.1888)

One time Mary reported:

> *Lord L.* (Lansdowne) *& the Duchess walked with me, & he told me all about his trees & plants in which he takes a great interest - the climate being so mild he is able to grow many things which only appear in greenhouses in England.* (12/6.9.1880)

Then she once wrote also that she had *talked to Lord Sherborne in the evening & we compared experiences of the discovery of plants.* (15/26.11.1889). There were also: *The Duke of Manchester announcing my Indian orchids,* (14/4.5.1887); *Lord Northbrook* (member of the wealthy Baring family) receiving from Mary *seed from the rockery of Anemone Pulsatilla,* (14/11.7.1886); and *Lord Walsingham giving me a list of plants found in the Esterels.* (14/17.4.1888). Significantly, all these, to whom Mary was friendly and sometimes deferential, were male aristocrats, more or less knowledgeable, and interested in the acquisition and display of plants. Whilst, temperamentally, it could be assumed she would have been equally happy to discuss with and take advice from other women, it is possible that there were few to rival her in interest or knowledge. On occasion, particularly as she grew older, Mary was able to reciprocate favours from her elite male interlocutors: *Wrote to the Secretary of the Working Men's Exhibition to Baron Ferdinand de Rothschild sending him 3 plants of Ferreya myrishea.* (14/16.10.1886)

Mary also wrote of head gardeners of other establishments, such as William Barron, who was commissioned by the Earl of Harrington to work on the grounds of Elvaston Castle, Derbyshire in the 1830s and achieved fame through his landscaping. She described how she made a visit *to Barron late gardener at Elvestone, called to see him & I took him* (Davie, one of her gardeners) *round to see the trees & got a good deal of interesting information from him.* (8/7.10.1868). A few years later she told how: *Mr. Dack came over & gave me a report of his conference yesterday with Gilbert Lord Exeter's kitchen gardener from which we hope to gain some hints.* (10/ 17.2.1876)

Occasionally Mary's own grounds at Orton hosted visitors. In March 1868, numbers of people availed themselves of a notice that the public would be admitted to see the grounds: *William let off some fireworks & lighted up the cloister with lamps.* (8/5.3.1868)

Others of lower ranks did not enjoy such privileges, but there was increasingly a shared public culture between middle and upper classes. This embraced shows and exhibitions, including the Great Exhibition of 1851, museums, libraries, the commercial world of nurseries and the culture of conspicuous consumption. It also encompassed an expanding print and literary culture, including multitudinous books on gardening and the great horticultural journals and magazines of the nineteenth century.

4 As intermediate spaces, variously populated but sometimes unpopulated, gardens could supply the frustrations but,

perhaps, more often the blessings, of retirement. A garden could be a social area for the resident family and for many visitors but could, by virtue of its size and compartmentalised structure, also provide opportunities for retreat. A personal diary often, by its nature, receives the outpourings of loneliness, and this is true also of Mary's diary which recounts not only her social meetings, but also her solitary reflections.

The Victorian garden did become increasingly compartmentalised, with a variety of enclosed gardens and buildings, often dedicated to different horticultural ends. At Uffington, for example, Mary refers repeatedly to many areas including orchards, hopfields, hayfield, stackyard, melon ground, mushroom house, mill house, hothouses and various flower gardens. Not only could this make the cultivation of plants more focused, but it also increased the number of enclosures for privacy and the sense of the garden as a dwelling with many rooms. There were spaces within the larger space, facilitating desires for escape and withdrawal. Women sometimes liked to linger or even hide in these smaller enclosed domains. Charlotte was comfortable by her south wall or in her favourite avenue. Mary, had many favourite spots. At twelve years of age, she recounted, *I sat in the apple tree in the middle of my garden and then read or rather looked over 'The Counties of England'.* (13.8.1834). However, for Mary, an impression of movement through the landscape is often stronger. She sought out social companions in the garden and used landmarks as staging posts. At Uffington, typically, these could include gravel walk, ice-house, spring, avenues and waterside spots.

Studies of privileged women in gardens in the eighteenth century have sometimes tended to present a negative picture of the environment of a country garden and the activity of gardening for women. Such feelings of discontent appear also in the reference by garden writer, Jane Loudon in 1851 to a newly wed acquaintance who needed Jane's encouragement to find pleasure in a country garden:

> *"I am sorry to hear that you felt chilled and depressed at the first appearance of the Manor-House; though I am not surprised that you found the room you were ushered into dark and cold, since you tell me that the windows are shaded by some lofty Scotch pines, which are certainly the most gloomy of all the vegetable race, and which must necessarily impede both the light and the warmth of the sun. You add that you are ten miles from a market-town, and at least seven from any visitable neighbours; that the kitchen-garden is a mile from the house and under the care of a cross old gardener, who cannot be displaced; that there is no separate flower-garden; and, in short, that if it were not for your affection for your husband, you would be miserable."*

As the nineteenth century progressed, however, many women were more positively joyful about their gardens and about the science of botany and their countryside explorations, and Mary would be foremost among them. This ran deeper than the mere feeling of wellbeing within the garden and an increased appreciation of Nature; there was also an investment in the seeking and development of self, and whatever it was that constituted the 'self', seems to have been able to find its balance, perhaps more easily in a garden than anywhere else. Mary demonstrates this most graphically in her expressions of relief whenever she could return to her garden following either stressful events in the outside world or demanding situations within her home. On such occasions, her consciousness of the natural processes of her garden would expand, soon overcoming her distress at the troublesome issues in her life, just as when, in late adolescence, she was under harsh criticism from adults for her behaviour, and ran out into the wind and rain to get relief. (7.12.1842)

The same spaces and physical environment could have very different meanings for different characters. Mary gardened in a wholehearted physical way, going out on freezing mornings to dig and weed laboriously, wielding common garden tools. She traversed the spaces of the garden repeatedly at a run or a gallop, her zest fully expressed in her diary. Her gaze was typically earthward and on the growing abundance of the land, rather than on the lights and shadows or the distant spires of neighbouring Burghley.

On a mundane level, Mary acknowledged happily the virtues of housewifery, as is apparent from her clear sense of duty to maintain neatness and attractiveness, especially in the gardens. This quality was admired in the gardens of others as when, in childhood, she visited Mrs. Easton, reporting: **We admired her garden which is remarkable for its neatness & the beauty of its flowers.** (17.8.1835). There was always an inclusion of the practical and unromantic aspects of gardening and she recorded as a child how she **bent sticks along the paths to keep the dahlias from being trampled upon.** (22.5.1834). The pattern continued through life as when she **went out early & took the dead geraniums & summer flowers out of my garden with the help of the 3 children who carried them away in their barrows.** (5/28.11.1860)

Possessing, at least in the first part of her marriage, the means to live in leisure, Mary nonetheless made herself habitually busy, whilst exercising considerable choice over her occupations. She made little mention of kitchens or cookery, preferring to spend her time in the garden, though she was fascinated by that traditional icon of the domesticity of high-class women, 'the still.' Despite the decline of this domestic feature, Mary wrote during her childhood at Uffington, *I went out after breakfast & picked mulberry leaves for my silk worms - The rest of the morning I spent in the still room.* (17.6.1835). During her marriage she clung to this fading custom: **Took him** (Mr. Marsh) **to the kitchen to see my little still at work, distilling Elder flower water.** (2/11.7.1851)

Fundamental also to Mary, as to most women, was the adornment of her home, not only as the mark of elegant leisure of an upper-class woman, but also to create care and homeliness. As a child, Mary **took up the geraniums** and recounted how she **potted them** and **brought them upstairs for the winter.** (17.10.1834). She told how **Lindsey & Elizabeth walked in the garden and brought home some Christmas with which they afterwards adorned the room.** (24.12.1834). Once, taking her cue to female behaviour from her mother, she **found Mama arranging the flowers & stayed up one hour later than usual to help her** (1.7.1836), and later in life she recorded typically how she *arranged flowers in the Dresden china vases for dinner.* (6/18.2.1862)

Mary, in the best traditions of housewifery, exchanged goods with friends and neighbours, most often in the form of bouquets, and she was happy both to give to those lower in social status and to receive from them, as in the following instances: *It was (a) very hot day and I and Elizabeth walked with Mrs Edmunds about the garden. I made a nosegay and gave it to her.* (21.2.1833); *Stopped at Edward Hubbard's house who gave me a beautiful bunch of primroses out of poor old Hubbard's garden.* (15.4.1835); *Eliza Betts was picking some cowslips to make cowslip tea. She gave me a cup of it after it was made- I thought it very good.* (23.4.1835); *Mary* (junior), *made a bouquet of white flowers & sent it over to Mrs. Cooke for her maid who is to be married this morning.* (5/16.10.1861). Being a gracious hostess was also a part of this domestic persona and a skill taught early in life. It was one in which Mary took pleasure as when *I heard Papa call me from the library window he told me as I was to take Miss Gordon (who had come here with her father) to walk about the garden and park.* (7.4.1834). The needs of immediate family were particularly important. In childhood, Mary *walked down the avenue and there found one of Charlotte's favourite white violets.* (29.1.1834); and when her mother was ill, *we arranged all little matters that could make her comfortable.* (11.8.1834)

Did their gardens construct women or the women, on the contrary, construct their gardens, or was this process mutual and interactive? It is now common to consider landscape, alongside other parts of the material world, as a 'text,' and this word has often been applied to eighteenth-century landscape gardens. These were designed to provide a tour for visitors, punctuated by classical allusions, which those possessing taste and culture could 'read' in the prescribed way. The notion of a text, however, can profitably be applied to any garden or landscape and here, specifically, to the way a woman both read and constructed her garden. Thus such gardens as these and the women who roamed and cultivated them are held in tension, in recognition that beyond the relative constancy of the actual landscape, the women to a large extent constructed the gardens for themselves. The travelling between landmarks was measured in desire, fantasy, imagination and the fulfilment of social needs, rather than in terms of classical allusion or politics. As demonstrated in her diary, Mary, like other such women in country houses and gardens, inscribed her own agenda upon the landscape, so that the topography acquired a powerful personal significance within the framework of horticultural collections and dynastic symbols.

Not only did different women construe gardens in different ways, but the same woman might reconfigure her garden in successive life stages. At Orton Manor, for example, both in the early days and, after her children were grown, Mary focused on her plant collections, her rockery, fernery and flower gardens. However, whilst raising her children, she conceived a family garden where the meadows served to educate her children about natural history. She once described her children plucking wildflowers for her from the Long Walk, which she later pressed (2/ 30.8.1851). Pathways were frequented which facilitated the family's life and leisure. As her husband's health was failing prior to his death, not only did she accommodate her perspective of the garden to the capabilities of an invalid, but she also worked with him to create symbols of dynasty, especially the Long Walk, the main avenue and approach to the mansion. Similarly she provided loving memorials for her deceased husband and children in Holy Trinity Church in the grounds of Orton, referring to them periodically in her diary.

Activity in, and enjoyment of, the garden usually represent the robust and healthy body. To begin, there was a fundamental physical relationship, with garden features becoming landmarks in personal development. As a young girl, Mary announced, *Papa promised me on the way that I should go out shooting with him tomorrow on the pony. I opened the park gates for my self arriving home.* (8.10.1834?). She also proudly reported *I opened six of the farm gates by myself and jumped over two ditches and a hedge.* (28.10.1834?). Thus the gates of Uffington Park are mentioned by Mary in the context of her early life, an example of how the history of self within the garden may be tied to events relating to material features. It is not clear which gates these were. Possibly they were the churchside gates, a miniature version of those referred to by Nikolaus Pevsner as *"the magnificent GATE-PIERS facing the churchyard, quite the best in the county"*. Pevsner conjectures that these may be by John Lumley, dated about 1700, mentioning *"tall rusticated brick piers faced with fluted stone pilasters and topped by urns with coronets"* and *"reversed scrolled brackets garlanded with fruit."* Alternatively, though with less likelihood, they may have been the main lodge gates or they may have been internal gates. Similarly, the avenue of Wellingtonias in the

Long Walk at Orton, which she helped her husband to make, has both monumental significance and also many contemporaneous personal meanings centring on her family life. This avenue still exists, though some trees are missing.

Most experiences of the garden recorded in diaries are comfortable and happy ones, but unpleasant and painful body experiences are also present. In a phenomenological account of gardens exploring imaginative engagement, we can perceive women as embodied individuals within large congenial spaces. Sensory experience could be vivid. At Aboyne, Mary physically touched and registered the pleasures of a sylvan scene when she was *glad to sit in the shade of the lime trees & pull out the grass from the tufts of wild thyme.* (4/10.10.1857). The connections between sensation and imagination could become crucial on occasions as when, a couple of years before her death:

> Mary (junior) *went to the rockery & brought back detailed accounts of the flowers now coming into beauty though unusually backward this year. The Daffodils only just out. I see them from my window & wish I could see them nearer, though I can see each plant on the rockery with my mind's eye.* (15/14.4.1891)

The body, so strongly linking the women to the material surroundings of landscape and garden with all their sensual offerings, often asserted itself very strongly. Mary's body was elated in traversing and cultivating her gardens though feeling many aches and pains when present in other locations, and also sometimes finding the limitations of her physical strength evenwithin her own gardens. In fact, for Mary, who displayed a marked tendency to react psychosomatically to life's stresses, the many descriptions in her diaries of headaches, sore throats and tiredness are oddly juxtaposed in her youth with the physical raptures of running or galloping through her gardens and vigorous engagement with soil and plants. On most of these occasions, the emotional causes of her feelings of unwellness came from outside the garden, but there was pain and sickness also heavily associated with pregnancy and child-bearing. As she lost strength towards the end of her life, the countryside and, even the garden, themselves became causative of further weakness. As early as 1862 she wrote: *Went out & attempted putting my garden in order - but it was too much for me.* (5/27.1.1862). In her latter days this became more of a theme. During her trip to the European Alps in middle age, she revealed, *I longed like a goat to skip from rock to rock & discover new beauties at every step.* (9/15.3.1871). A couple more entries that year echo this: *The pursuit of plants was conducted under difficulties.* (9/11.7.1871); *Searching for plants as far as my strength would carry me.* (9/29.7.1871). Nearly fifteen years later, she described rocks *covered with ferns & other vegetation rejoicing beneath the trickling water which one would give anything for in a rockery* but then reported that she *got out once to look for plants but found I could not scramble.* (13/26.5.1885). A few years later she wrote: *I had not much strength for scrambling.* (14/20.3.1888). Some years after this she stated in resignation, *I wished I could have seen more of this wild ground & the wood beyond but must be thankful for even my limited powers.* (15/27.7.1892)

Fashionable practice is sometimes apparent in the gardening preoccupations of women. The pursuit of botany had remained prominent in female culture since the eighteenth century and this was associated with an enthusiasm for native plants, especially those that were first of the season or rare. Mary's almost obsessional interest in native plants flowed between the simple love of picking and distributing bunches of them to the sophistication of scientific botany. One of her endlessly repeated operations was the digging up of roots in the wild to replant in the flower beds in her gardens, as when she went to the woods as a child and *dug up a large basket of primroses & orchises... Planted the primroses in the new shrubberies & the orchises in my own garden.* (18.3.1837). Much later at Orton, the Long Walk was also adorned with native plants, as innumerable flowers from the wild and from other parts of the garden were transplanted there. Once Mary went to Haddon Nursery and *filled the donkey cart with ferns & early purple orchises which we planted on either side of the new carriage road at the end of the Long Walk.* (5/5.5.1860). The interest in wildflowers, especially, linked her to the succession of seasons, as she ran out to find violets, primroses and mushrooms, reaping the bounties of nature at anticipated times.

This was supplemented with a long-lasting interest in ferns which coincided with a fashionable craze beginning mid-century. Mary collected and planted ferns on the Scottish estate and used some of the Scottish ferns, to make a fernery at Orton, extending her use of these plants to decorative garden arrangements and to Wardian cases, which were invented in the 1820s by Nathaniel

Bagshaw, initially for preserving plants during sea voyages, and subsequently becoming fashionable for use in homes.

Alternating with the passion for native plants was a celebration of exotics, especially those newly imported or rare. The acquisition of these enhanced status and this was often linked with excitement about the riches of Empire. Mary supported her husband's interest in imported conifers and shared with him an interest in the exploits of the great plant-hunters. She once wrote: **On S's return read to him some accounts of plants from Fortune's wanderings in China.** (2/25.10.1852). And, as noted in the last chapter, her own relatives brought her foreign plants from their travels.

Facilitating the cultivation of exotics was the growth of glasshouse technologies. Flower decoration, indoor arrangements and Wardian cases also became fashionable. There is no evidence that Mary left England until after the death of her husband and, when she finally did travel to Europe, much of her time was spent in collecting plants to add to her rock garden at home which assumed increasing importance towards the end of her life. The creation of rock gardens was also a very fashionable pursuit, but Mary excelled in it. Typically she wrote: **Found to my great delight gentiana verna in flower in my rockery - a plant brought 2 years ago from the Pyrenees.** (8/21.4.1870)

There were some fundamental differences in the roles played by reading and gardening in Mary's life. For example, whilst she was intensely engaged with both, it was the latter which involved her physical engagement i.e. her embodiment, and initially was the greater draw. The healthy and even hardworking body fostered by gardening activity strengthened feelings of assertiveness, a consequence perhaps unintended by those who directed women towards the garden in order to keep them 'harmlessly' absorbed; and, generally, for English upper-class women, the garden seemed to produce a certain hardiness which was apparent in Mary's enthusiastic digging as a child on freezing winter days. Exertion and dirty hands did not always seem so amiss especially for those in the higher echelons, who had the potential to be less conformist.

Whilst Mary, not only by education and cultural influences, but also by inclination, was always a keen and discriminating reader, sometimes reading came more into its own at times of physical weakness, such as illness, pregnancy or old age, or because of environmental adversity such as harsh weather. Of course, the appreciation of the natural world and of books often coincided as Mary and children sat reading in the garden. Also, although reading seemingly involves more thinking and gardening more feeling, the best books and the best natural experiences involve both. Thought aroused feeling and as Mary gardened, her intellectual faculties were alive. All in all, despite their alternate appearance in Mary's time, and their functioning as complementary activities, her modus operandi in both activities, on close analysis, shows many similarities, both in motivations and characteristics.

MOTIVATIONS

Consumerism

Mary experienced her plants as a form of wealth. She plundered the countryside, gathering armfuls of flowers, sometimes also providing them as gifts. Before her marriage, she reported herself *in the garden picking flowers in the rain* which she described as *my valueless valuables.* (11.6.1843). Many years later, at Ascot, Mary wrote, *The day was glorious & I rejoiced in a sight of the country & red poppies & corn flowers more than the gay toilettes assembled for the races.* (10/19.6.1874). She had the desire, extending to greed, to pluck and possess in abundance flowers, butterflies and other such delights, feasting on them with her eyes, grasping them with her hands. On one occasion, when the young Mary was travelling in Wales, others enacted her acquisitiveness for her:

> *En route with the addition to our cavalcade of a guide, two men, with cloaks and provision, & a couple of ragged little urchins, who discovering by instinct my love of flowers brought me handful after handful of heaths & honeysuckle.* (30.8.1843)

The constant desire to walk and work in her gardens and later to scour the Alps for plants for her rockery, continued right through and to the end of her life. After leaving her much-loved childhood garden of Uffington, her fortunate position as wife and then widow of the 10th Marquis of Huntly endowed her with beautiful gardens both at her home at Orton Hall and the family's Scottish Estate at Aboyne Castle in Aberdeenshire. These were the free and bounteous gifts attendant upon the position to which she was born and into which she married. Flowers were her treasure, not only those in her own gardens, but those of the countryside and, generally unsolicitous of worldly treasures, she grasped eagerly at these. *Walked with Strath to the stables to see Tippoo & gathered violets in the shrubberies.* (1/10.4.1844); *Took a walk with dear Strath & explored to the end of the long walk where we gathered a basket full of cowslips & returned by the Park.* (1/18.4.1844); *Gathered flowers in the garden some sprays of the penstemon, & two or three flowers of the... which is now in full beauty.* (1/6.5.1844)

Also:

> *I was delighted with my first view of the beautiful forest, and my admiration increased the further we penetrated into it. We soon discovered the place where the lilies of the valley grow and their luxuriance exceeded by far my anticipations. We gathered the flowers, but deferred the more laborious work of digging up the roots till the day should be cooler, & having reached the centre tree, & discovered a small opening in the adjoining dingle, we unloaded the gig of a large basket of provisions, sitting down upon our cloaks.* (1/13.5.1844)

In some women's diaries, there is a strong sense of idyll conveyed by descriptions of their gardens, especially in childhood. These could be large and often beautiful pieces of ground surrounding expensive properties. Sadly and ironically the gardens over which they presided were sometimes 'endangered paradises,' subject to the adverse effects of current social and economic conditions and human failings and, ultimately, in many cases, at this time of political and economic and climatic change, the march to bankruptcy.

Alongside the enjoyment of the gardens, a competitive spirit, based on pride in possession, often prevailed amongst women and Mary was not exempt from this. Whilst this might be at odds with the benign domestic ideal of womanhood, few were immune to the temptation to show off their gardens. 'Improvements' are often referred to in Mary's diary and others. Mary herself was unusually lacking in vanity, but always pleased nonetheless to show to admiring visitors the rockery she had made and the Wellingtonia Avenue and conifer collection she had helped her husband to create. In her declining years, she grew more competitive, taking particular pleasure in the prize awarded her by the Royal Horticultural Society and the awarding to her of the Veitch Memorial Medal.

Whilst Charlotte appeared to enjoy extended periods of travel, Mary's energies were always focused on home and bringing the treasures of the world within its bounds: **Lovely plant-wished could be transported to rockery.** (13/22.4.1885). Although she took some trips to Europe in later years, she spent much of the time making contacts with other botanists and exploring mountainous regions for plants to take back to her rockery. This was the brightest part of her garden where the world bloomed

THE RELUCTANT ARISTOCRAT ~ 217

and where she made sunshine for herself and her family. She worked there mostly alone but sometimes with her children; she sojourned there with visitors and sat there with her grandchildren. She also built rockeries in the homes of her children. Her interest was both instinctive and sentimental but also clearly scientific in view of her dedicated practices of plant collection and classification. In her garden she had a small replica of the alps and she resorted to her rockery when all else was failing. She planted and weeded assiduously, and here her labours eventually amounted to the fabled activity of 'arranging the deckchairs on the Titanic;' her diary and herbarium and the remains of the rockery did however outlast the financial disaster which finally overtook the estates.

Relatives and friends also brought her plants from abroad, feeding into the current taste for exotics and excitement about the riches of Empire. Note the following: *Went with Davie to see the oaks in the wilderness which we suppose to be grown from the acorn brought by H Layard from Kurdistan 1850* (7/5.12.1864); *Mary helped me to arrange dried ferns- & also the collection of plants collected by Henry Layard in Kurdistan.* (7/8.2.1865); *Sorting the Syrian plants.* (7/11.2.1865); *Nineveh plants among my dried collection.* (7/17.7.1865); *Over the grounds with H. Layard & showed him the oaks grown from the acorns he brought back from the East- the Wellingtonias conifers & rock garden.* (7/18.7.1865); *Sir James Hogg with a packet of Indian seeds of conifers.* (7/1.5.1866); *Thanking Mr Boyle for his seeds from the Mauritius.* (7/3.5.1866); *Out on the lawn and looked at the Syrian oaks in the wilderness.* (8/7.7.1867); *Looked through the dried plants brought by Henry Layard from Nineveh.* (13/

6.2.1883). The same year at Orton, she walked over the grounds with (General) Frederic Layard who was *much pleased with the rockery & collection of plants growing upon it, and described how he went through a number of my botanical books comparing some of the specimens with his drawings which he found wrongly named.* (13/14.11.1883). Six years later, she went *Over the grounds with Henry Layard & Harding who took us to see oak trees grown, as we think from acorns sent by H.L from the East years ago.* (15/23.3.1889). A couple of years after this, she wrote to *Edgar Layard asking him to remember me if he should meet with rare plants in Devonshire.* (15/6.2.1891). Edgar was another of Mary's cousins and a colonial administrator who, amongst a number of countries, spent some time in South Africa, becoming, in 1855, Curator of the South African Museum. Mary's gardener contributed to the discussion: *Harding quoted information he has received from the books of travel respecting conifers in their native countries.* (14/2.1.1887)

Reading, in quite a similar way, was a process of bringing into the intellectual and cultural store of her mind, treasures from the outside- treasures which were sometimes shared in conversation and in education of her children, servants and the workers, mothers and children on her estates. Books were also objects of consumption and similarly might be read in a competitive spirit. Although there were many serious reasons for reading, they were also there to fill leisure hours, especially during long years of widowhood.

Fashion

Mary, as has been seen, despite her unworldliness, pursued both reading and gardening in a fashion-conscious way: that is she went with the flow, consistent with the compliant personality that prevailed in her post-adolescent years. Her activities in the garden follow quite closely the stages in the fashion of the times: the creating of a rock garden, the making also of a fern garden, production of mini foreign landscapes, the bringing in of exotics. Mary followed the common pattern but undertook all this with great passion and to an excellent standard.

Her reading also followed fashionable lines. She used Mudie's and other circulating libraries and read works, just published, of a progressive or controversial nature, influenced by the intelligent circles in which she moved but, as with gardening and botany, she embraced these activities in a dedicated way, showing unusual breadth and depth of reading.

Educational activity

A further link is the educational one. Mary's botany turned into a lifelong study and a hunt in Europe for plants which she documented and entered into her herbarium. Her observations were supplemented by consultation with experts who were often, coincidentally her friends. All this became incorporated in her education of her children.

Huntly wrote, "My mother's chief object in making these collections was to imbue her children with a love of nature."

Similarly, her reading often fed directly into their education, so books were often selected for this purpose.

Escape

The act of 'escape' is a common factor in both reading and garden activities. The need for peace and withdrawal has already been discussed in relation to the garden, but this clearly also characterises some kinds of reading - e.g. in the gratification of fantasy offered by romantic novels, but also in the space to study and come to grips with intellectual and academic studies. In fact, as already noted, books and gardens often conspired together to provide opportunities for escape as, in good weather, reading might take place in the garden. For Mary, reading was a particularly necessary form of escape after the death of her husband, especially as her physical strength was declining and she suffered more prolonged periods of illness.

Both reading and gardening, the one primarily mental, the other physical and sensuous, also represented some freedom from the straitjacket of Victorian life, with the opportunity, for extensive exploration; perhaps for Mary, also, they were diversions from the inexorable financial problems and the threatened loss of lands.

Play/Psychological Balance

In her youthful years, especially, Mary's zest overflowed in many forms of playfulness and the gardens formed a world she was reluctant to leave even as she grew up. Note the eleven year old Mary at play with sister Elizabeth at Uffington:

> *We went out after dinner with the intention of working at Lindsey's garden. But soon found we were more in a mode play than work for we got up some sticks and danced with these; we then went to the garden where we strolled about till 5 o'clock.* (17.2.1834)

Through most of her diaries, especially the early ones, such lighthearted themes predominate in the context of the garden. Thus, a day later, Mary told how they, *played about out of doors and got a fir tree which we turned upside down and put Mr. Farmer's cap on the top.* (18.2.1834). Note also the zest and humour in Mary's description, as a young adult, of a riding incident in the grounds of Uffington House: *The stirrup gave way I lost my balance and came rolling down a bank laughing aloud at each involuntary somersault.* (8.3.1843). Through changing circumstances, spatial freedom and play could also support a volatile self. There was the potential within seemingly limitless spaces, for grandiose notions of self but, at the other extreme, the garden could shrink in perception almost to the dimensions of a flower or insect, especially when viewed through the eyes of the natural historian, or when fortunes and pride were diminishing. In the midst of disaster, Mary remained proud spirited whilst being stripped of the trappings of status. As her material wealth declined, she started to wish fervently for a quiet retreat into an inconspicuous lifestyle: *Got no rest at night & feel disposed to go away & leave it all & to live in the smallest means in obscurity.* (13/8.5.1883). Learning to adapt and cope with the permutations of self could be a rehearsal for the outside world or a therapeutic replaying of its traumas.

Books were also a source of humour and playfulness. Even after the shock of losing her sister in childhood, Mary was able to find release in laughter as she read Dickens' *Pickwick Papers*: **Began reading Pickwick Papers & was greatly entertained** ... (15.4.1837), and her reading was always leavened with light-hearted and funny texts.

Work

Whilst playfulness and humour could be aspects both of reading and gardening, so also could hard work. Mary did work hard in her garden, even undertaking extensive weeding, despite the lower-class connotations of this activity and the availability of gardeners. As she grew older and less fit, she struggled with this physical work.

She also applied herself assiduously to her books and occasionally struggled with them though she rarely gave up.

CHARACTERISTICS

Christian Worship

Everything Mary did was permeated by her Christianity; this was the primary characteristic of all as well as a powerful motivator. Her love of Nature in garden and wilderness was imbued with the perception of God as Creator. Her reading was primarily religious in nature.

Absence of Strategy

> "Women are by nature conservative; they cling to the past, and to anything that reminds them of the past .... If men take to gardening, this leads to revolution among the flower-beds, and results in the loss of many old favourites .... In a woman's garden "pretty bits" and individually attractive flowers will be likely to catch the eye, rather than the general effect of the whole ... a jumble of bright colours, but when examined carefully is found to be full of interest ... a lady gardener will allow her affections to twine themselves round particular paths, colours, or trees;..."

Whilst this piece from *Gardeners' Chronicle* may appear to be a sexist account, in line with most nineteenth-century accounts of gender differences, nonetheless it seems true that, most frequently for women, neither reading nor gardening was strategic. Although she operated at a high level, with seriousness and skill, there was little strategy involved in Mary's practice of either. Her gardens were not design entities, or at least were not designed by her, but a lived experience full of walks, conversations, events, games, animals, birds, pets and, most of all, beautiful plants. A different story should be told of Mary's botanical work which she performed in very strategic fashion, classifying family after family of plants to produce a herbarium which would be amply praised by botanists Sheail and Wells.

Her reading also, for similar reasons, generally followed a random pattern, covering a variety of subjects, influenced by many forces, and not subject to any preconceived programme, so that the compartmental structure of her mind mirrored that of her garden. Again, this was not necessarily the case with the educational provision for children and servants which was normally carried out in a highly strategic manner.

Recycling

In the cultivation of plants, there were social chains to supplement the natural cycles. The sequence of events could go from the family expedition, to the gathering of seeds or roots, planting in the garden, nurturing, plucking, arranging in vases, or tying into bunches and dispatching to a destination, maybe a flower show or the home of a sick friend. For Mary, as for many Victorian women, flowers played a profound social and emotional role: *It was a very hot day and I and Elizabeth walked with Mrs Edmunds about the garden. I made a nosegay and gave it to her.*

(21.2.1833); *Stopped at Edward Hubbard's house who gave me a beautiful bunch of primroses out of poor old Hubbard's garden.*(15.4.1835); *Eliza Betts was picking some cowslips to make cowslip tea. She gave me a cup of it after it was made - I thought it very good.* (23.4.1835)

Books went through a similar process; beyond the stages of their production, they were acquired from different sources, read and passed on in various ways- lent to others, discussed in conversation, involved in educational activity.

Prescription

Of course, for women, both reading and gardening, were subject to prescriptive forces, which tended to inhibit both action and expression but did not always succeed in doing so. Innumerable gardening books told women how to be ladylike in the garden, gracefully planting and nurturing but not over exerting themselves or taking initiative in design and landscaping.

Similarly, many, including clergy, were keen to warn women against reading material thought likely to corrupt them. The emphatic way in which this advice was usually delivered, indicates that it was felt to be a losing battle, as the novel and feminist literature rose to prominence.

Sociability

Although Mary, in childhood, often gardened alone, she described a joyous social life in the garden at Uffington, and also at Orton and Aboyne- particularly in earlier more carefree times.

Reading could also take place in a spirit of companionship, with reading aloud sessions and the books that created excitement passed from one to another.

6

Woman Amongst Women

The generality of the male sex cannot yet tolerate the idea of living with an equal.
(Mill, *The Subjection of Women*, 1870) p.91. (1869) (8/ 22.5.1870)

Thanksgiving to God for his great goodness in giving me so dear & valuable a protector and this happy peaceful house.
Mary's Diaries (1/23.4.1844)

Despite the accelerating influence of feminism during the nineteenth century, Mary, like many women at this time, was accepting of and reasonably content with her lot, and felt her somewhat submissive status to be not only appropriate, but also divinely ordained. The following factors, however, should be considered:

1 She was of the aristocracy and much less oppressed than other groups of women. Much of the daily work of a landed gentleman was on site in his country house and estate, so home and work were not necessarily separated. As she entered motherhood, the Marquis was frequently away hunting whilst Mary was personally absorbed in the nurture and later the education of her children to a degree not traditional amongst the aristocracy. Nonetheless, these were circumstances with which she was absolutely comfortable and did not represent any form of gender oppression.

2 Mary was generally fortunate in her circumstances, both materially and in her social position, especially in the early years of her marriage, though there was some decline later. Her attitude was one of gratitude rather than rebellion.

3 Mary had a calm, contented, largely unambitious personality. During adolescence she obediently, though reluctantly, conformed to the expectations of society to present a comely and cheerful face to the world, turning to self-reproach when she fell short in this regard. She was happy to accept the advances of Lord Strathavon, a much older man, considered herself fortunate in doing so and was loving and deferential throughout the marriage although, on his death, a long and difficult widowhood awaited her.

4 **Mary had a warm and, for the most part, happy relationship with her husband.** The sense that she was being groomed for marriage seemed to distress her in adolescence, but the reality did not justify the dread. Although Strath was sometimes critical of her, he was a kind and companionable mate. In the following passage from his diary, where he describes the difference in their botanical tastes, manifest at a horticultural show, the tone is affectionate:

> "With Mary to the botanical gardens... Palms, Bananas fine grown specimens of Pinus, Berberis splendid Irish Yews, the largest Araucaria - I ever saw Mary enchanted with Verbascums Sedums, Centaureas, Ferns, Veronicas, & co - I could hardly keep her hand from picking & stealing." Marquis's Diary (23.7.1846)

Writing once from Scotland, Strath told his wife:

> "Found the little Vetch in full flower the root of which I fancy I have heard you say the highlander used to eat or cook? ... I send you a bit but I fear it will be all squeezed to pieces before you get it." (4.6.1851)

5 **Mary's half-sister, Charlotte fought hard, both to maintain and advance her aristocratic status and for empowerment as a woman. Mary perceived herself as very different,** especially in view of some of the unconventional, and even scandalous, decisions made by Charlotte, which Mary thought selfish. Although

affection ultimately developed between them, Mary was never tempted to see Charlotte as a role model although she did sometimes pay her generous tribute, as in the year prior to her own marriage: *How wonderful she is! Always ready to work with body (and) mind, however unequal from weakness or fatigue.* (12.5.1843)

Mary's notions of ideal womanhood were somewhat divergent from those of Charlotte, whose more highly aristocratic status may have given her added confidence to cross boundaries. Charlotte was a loyal wife and good mother of ten children, but ventured beyond these female 'normalities' to take on a variety of less socially sanctioned roles, running the ironworks after her husband's death, translating, founding schools, travelling abroad to collect fans, pottery and porcelain and games. She broke with convention in both her marriages, in the first marrying an industrialist rather than fellow-aristocrat, still not entirely acceptable, and in her second, taking a partner, not only younger, but also beneath her in the social scale- her son's tutor. She ignored the wishes of her family in these matters and seemed to care little for their disapproval. Both were shocking to Mary, although her attitude to Charlotte later softened.

These are a few of Mary's entries relating to the furore over Charlotte's liaison with her future second husband: *Heard from H.L. a very sad account of the state of things at Canford! Can it be true?* (3/8.1.1855); *Heard from Papa & H.L. They had conferred together respecting the Canford affair & both take a gloomy view of things.* (3/30.1.1855)

Also:

> About 12 'Lady Charlotte Guest' was announced. I went down to the drawing room to her & we talked for an hour. She evidently wished me to announce the event to Mama & the world generally putting the best face upon it but I told her I wished to have nothing to do with it. The revelation deeply grieved me & I was much affected but her manner was that of a person who had long made up their mind & was prepared to sacrifice every body & every thing to obtain one object ... Could not rest at night thinking of this affair. (3/9.2.1855)

> Met ... Lady Hall who, as did many others, attacked me about Charlotte (in a conversation at the Queen's ball). (3/1.6.1855)

6 **Mary was guided by her religion** and the virtues of humility, dutifulness, unworldliness, and the 'separate spheres' philosophy- inapplicable as these sometimes were to her circumstances. These taught her submission to her husband and a focus on a maternal, domestic role, and writers such as Ruskin and innumerable clergy and other influential male and female writers reinforced the message:

> "Indeed it is amongst my heaviest afflictions, the feeling myself incapable of the duties of wife and mother: this admits of but one consolation, that though David was not permitted to build the temple of the Lord, yet it was accepted, for he had

it in his heart." (Hare, A., *Memorials of a Quiet Life.*, 1873) p.150 (1872). (9/21.8.1873)

7 **Some of the possible associations of feminism at this time would have been unattractive to Mary** e.g. loud, coarse, self-assertive behaviour and independence of the guidance and provision of men.

8 **Much current literature, especially fiction, was of middle-class origin,** so Mary absorbed many bourgeois values. These exposed her to the 'separate spheres' model of life. Her favourite preacher, Frederick Robertson, amongst others, subscribed to a chivalric and separatist view of women:

> "There is one glory of manhood, and another glory of womanhood. And the glory of each created thing consists in being true to its own nature, and moving in its own sphere." (Robertson, *Sermons*, 2nd Series, 1855 - 18 *The First Miracle*) (Robertson, *Sermons Preached at Brighton, by the late Rev. Frederick W. Robertson*, New York: Harper, 1905) p. 395. (1860 onwards)

9 **The genre of prescriptive literature targeted especially at middle-class women** not only told women whether and what they should read, but sometimes linked general social behaviour with specific contexts such as gardening practices and the pursuit of botany, so that advice on how a young lady should behave in the drawing room was supplemented by similar advice on what she could appropriately do in the garden or in the

countryside. Note the following piece, one of many on the same topic, from the *Gardeners' Chronicle*:

> "We must not pretend to be too scientific, lest the gentlemen should call us to account for trespassing on their domain; but we must do our best to understand what appertains to our botanical province lest, on the other hand, the trowels be torn from our grasp, and we ourselves be once more consigned to needles and thread ... We might buy a modest little volume on the subject."

All was in a similar vein of encouraging virtuous and ladylike behaviour and discouraging high aspiration.

10 Fear of social disapproval played a part. Whilst Mary was largely able to disregard this in most situations, it sometimes had a wearing effect upon her self-esteem.

On one occasion, Mary received an unexpected visit from a haughty acquaintance: **Lady Westmoreland called & I had to come in gardening attire to receive her.** (5/10.4.1860). Three decades later she was at the **rockery with Mr Marsh & Nellie who insisted upon watering the flowers ... & stained her pelisse much to Mrs Brown's disgust.** (15/2.5.1890)

It would have taken more self-assertion than Mary possessed not to be, at least a little, intimidated by such socially oppressive and largely sexist attitudes, especially when demonstrated by other women. She suffered many minor ailments such as sore throats and headaches some of which seem suspiciously psychosomatic; so it is possible that when she bent herself to compliance with social norms, this could have subconscious repercussions.

Like women of all classes, Mary was subject to patronizing remarks relating to her gender and reactionary comments on her aspirations, but tolerated most of them well. For example, although changing fashions in gardening, such as the craze for rock and fern gardens, as well as the intensification of existing practices like botanical collecting, could offer women more scope for creativity or scholarly accomplishment, ironically they could also feed into further stereotypes and patronizing attitudes. Mary, despite her advanced botanical skills and growing accomplishments, often seemed oblivious to this.

Once, she:

> made a large collection of cup lichens which are just now in great beauty & one particularly abundant in this locality. Dr. Adams had called in the morning & told me it was almost impossible for an amateur to name the cryptogamous plants. (3/13. 10. 1855)

The following year, she described a visit to the botanical gardens and recorded that:

> Mr McNab was most civil & obliging & gave me specimens from the fern collection which interested me very much.

> *He accused me by saying, that 'Ferns' was one of the things that Ladies appeared to know more about than gentlemen & that therefore they were anxious to display their knowledge.* (3/29.10.1856)

Later in her life, the following is recorded, though Mary's feisty second daughter was more equal to the occasion:

> **Lord Clarendon expressed his disapproval of women's speaking in public which drew forth some amusing descriptions, Evy defending her speeches at the meetings of the Primrose League.** (15/18.8.1889)

Furthermore, Mary, in her timid and unsuccessful attempts to get her writing published, as described in Chapter 1, probably owed her difficulties not only to any lack of talent or confidence but also to the discouragement encountered perpetually by aspiring female authors.

Mary internalised misogyny at a certain level, and responded more to individual extreme instances of it than in any general or systematic way. When women's role was discussed, she could enter dispassionately into the conversation: **Had an interesting conversation with L. Blanche about Arnold & his opinions, & the various paths of usefulness open to woman.** (1/27.11.1848), though after reading a biography of clergyman Richard Cecil, an ardent advocate of separate spheres, she wrote, **His opinion of the female character is far from flattering** (3/28.9.1856). When unable to deal with servants, Mary gratefully solicited the authority of her husband to enforce her wishes and her 'failures' in this regard, if they should be so called, are well documented in Chapter 1.

She read and was, no doubt, influenced by the works of a number of 'empowered' women who, despite impressive profiles, were strangely apologetic about stepping outside their prescribed role:

> "*I have given him the book, and hope to find answers for all his petty objections. It is safe to look for them in good writers, and unsafe and unseemly, perhaps, in a woman to enter the lists of controversy herself.*" (Trench, *The Remains of the Late Mrs. Richard Trench*, 1862) p.391-392. (6/25.9.1862)

> "*But it is not merely in particular acts, but in the whole manner and tone of feeling, that true gentle womanliness should manifest itself; and might not my present employment, which necessitates some occupation with books and scientific knowledge, have an injurious influence in this respect?*" (Poel, *Life of Amelia Wilhelmina Sieveking*, 1863) p.47. (6/2.1.1864)

> "*If I had to begin life over again I would marry, because a woman ought to live with a man, and to be in subjection.*" (Lonsdale, *Sister Dora: A Biography*, 1888) p.40. (1881). (15/21.11.1889)

In view of the self-denigration even of these notable women, it is not surprising that Mary felt some intimidation.

If anything should have evoked a more powerful response in Mary, it would have been the discouragement she met in the downward trajectory of her life, from businessmen and relatives, with even her own children sometimes talking over the top of her; but she appeared to take this as the natural course of things for a woman, and sometimes to accept it as a form of chastening. She seemed unresentful of her predicament, though devastated by it.

Her extensive reading exposed her to a number of different models of womanhood, both those which reinforced her own attitudes and those which contradicted them. There were, for example, both in her reading of novels and non-fiction, many examples of the 'good woman' set forth as a role model. (Here, and throughout the chapter, fictional characters give voice to social viewpoints and may or may not express the views of the authors of the works.)

> "Thus, in literature, as in other things, and especially in domestic life, has the mercy of God bestowed on woman the especial and distinguishing blessing of upholding the moral and religious influence, that spirit of truth and love by which man can alone be redeemed from the fall she brought upon him." (Schimmelpenninck; Hankin, *Life of Mary Ann Schimmelpenninck*, 1860) vol 1, p.125. (1858) (5/7.11.1860)

> "Ruth's love seemed to have flung a cloak of purity about him that shielded and protected him." (Sims, *Rogues and Vagabonds*, 1885) p.223. (13/25.7.1885)

Frequently the narrative shows a woman in 'error' striving to attain the status of a 'good' woman:

> "She had to compel herself into sudden quietness, for her husband's sake, which, indeed, was a lesson now daily being learned, and growing every day sweeter in the learning." (Craik, *Christian's Mistake*, 1865) p.109. (New York: Harper). (7/4.4.1865)

> "She had been taken out of all her misery, and placed in the safe shelter of a good man's love." (Craik, *Christian's Mistake*, 1865) p.247. (New York: Harper). (7/4.4.1865)

> "She was too little unsexed, still too much of the woman, and she gave up the struggle. ... She descended to the level of ordinary humanity with but a small faith in its adequacy to content her. ... Still there was left her own life with its round of responsibilities and pleasures; senses were not dulled nor was the conscience cold. She must resign herself to the drift of necessity; ....and after years would find her less resentful of her fate, nay, perhaps even smiling at her younger enthusiasm, and fulfilling some of those positions of wife, sister, daughter, and mother ... to be able to say that one has been some of these well, and on the whole happily." (Watson, *Lady Faintheart*, 1890) vol 3, p.307. (15/3.6.1891)

> "Your wife adores you, and will try to follow as you lead. Be merciful, and don't attempt to wind up her slighter nature

to the height of your own. Make her as good as you can, but according to the faculties and bias God has given her; encourage and praise her, even beyond her deserts,- it is the breath of life to a woman,- and she will end in grasping what is now beyond her reach." (Needell, *Unequally Yoked*, 1891) p.379. (15/23.11.1891)

Thus Mary, partly because of the bias in her selection of texts, encountered a conservative model of woman, again often put forward by female authors, with which she would most likely feel identified, even though it was characteristically middle class. She would have found similar examples in such texts as: Edgeworth, *Lazy Lawrence and Simple Susan*; Sewell, *The Experience of Life*; Gordon, *Work or Plenty to Do*; Stephen, *Passages from the Life of a Daughter at Home*.

However, she was also frequently presented in her reading with alternative models, ironically also emanating from the middle classes. At the 'lower' end, at least so far as public esteem was concerned, was the notion of the 'fallen woman', one for which the term 'model' can be applied only in a very restricted sense. Mary once *heard from Felicia asking me to patronise with her a 'Female home.'* (3/12.12.1854). Years later she *received from Lady Welby a list of books & an address delivered at the inaugural meeting of the Grantham District Association for the care and help of girls & young women.* (14/25.1.1886)

Pious references appear in her reading, like the following:

> "The Sisterhood began its labors by endeavouring to receive and reclaim fallen women, a work which in conjunction with many others, it still retains." (Ashwell; Wilberforce, *Life of the Right Reverend Samuel Wilberforce*, 1880-1883) vol 3, p.322. (13/12.10.1883)

This figure of the fallen woman appeared in many sermons and novels of male and female authorship and was one of almost universal condemnation. The 'fallen' condition was usually regarded as irreversible, though compassion was often called for. It was central to Anthony Trollope's *Vicar of Bullhampton*:

> "Thus arises that further question,- how far the condition of such unfortunates should be made a matter of concern to the sweet young hearts of those whose delicacy and cleanliness of thought is a matter of pride to so many of us." (Trollope, *The Vicar of Bullhampton*, 1870) p.vi. (13/21.3.1884)

> "But no care, nothing that can be done by friends on earth, or even by better friendship from above, can replace that when once displaced." (Trollope, *The Vicar of Bullhampton*, 1870) pp.167-168. (13/21.3.1884)

> "Almost every family has a black sheep, and it is the especial duty of a family solicitor to keep the family black sheep from being dragged into the front and visible ranks of the

family." (Trollope, *The Vicar of Bullhampton*, 1870) p.195. (13/21.3.1884)

"The glory of the flower had been destroyed by the unworthy hand that had ravished its sweetness", (Trollope, *The Vicar of Bullhampton*, 1870) p.234. (13/21.3.1884)

"And it is useful. It keeps women from going astray." (Trollope, *The Vicar of Bullhampton*, 1870) p.237. (13/21.3.1884)

"He asked her whether she did not hate the disgrace and the ignominy and the vile wickedness of her late condition." (Trollope, *The Vicar of Bullhampton*, 1870) p.242. (13/21.3.1884)

"If ever Mary were to be so loved again that she might be given away, a long time might first elapse; and then she was aware that such gifts given late lose much of their value, and have to be given cheaply." (Trollope, *The Vicar of Bullhampton*, 1870) p.411. (13/21.3.1884)

Also, the following comment and questions appear later in Trollope's autobiography, generally advocating pity and help for these women, whilst remaining judgmental:

"I have endeavoured to explain that though there was possible to her a way out of perdition, still things could not be with her as they would have been had she not fallen." (Trollope, *An Autobiography*, 1883) p.177. (13/25.2.1884)

> "*Cannot women who are good pity the sufferings of the vicious, and do something, perhaps, to mitigate and shorten them, without contamination from the vice?*" (Trollope, An Autobiography, 1883) p.178. (13/25.2.1884)

> "*She is what she is, and she remains in her abject, pitiless, unutterable misery, because this sentence of the world has placed her beyond the helping hand of Love and Friendship*" (Trollope, An Autobiography, 1883) p.179. (13/25.2.1884)

> "*How is the woman to return to decency to whom no decent door is opened? Then comes the answer: it is to the severity of the punishment alone that we can trust to keep women from falling. And a quivering fear of that coming hell which still can hardly be worse than all that is suffered here! But for our erring sons we find pardon easily enough!*" (Trollope, An Autobiography, 1883) p.182. (13/ 25.2.1884)

Frederick Farrar referred obliquely to the situation of the fallen woman:

> "*To be restrained from suicide only by the certainty that your death must drive your helpless daughters to swell the ghastly army of degraded womanhood.*" (Farrar, Social and Present Day Questions, 1891) pp. 83-84. (15/22.5.1892)

There were, nonetheless, questionings by both male and

female writers of the double standard.

> "We have one law of morality for men, and another law for women." (Vaughan, *Lessons of life and Godliness*, 1862) p.230. (6/9.11.1862)

> "There is one sex, at least, with which the one wrong step is irretraceable. What disproportionate punishment often follows on little acts of haste or folly!" (Boyd, *The Commonplace Philosopher in Town and Country*, 1864). p.169. (6/ 9.5.1864)

In the novel *The Heavenly Twins* by Sarah Grand, read by Mary in her final year of life, the double standard of morality was emphatically questioned:

> "You meant to marry always," she said, "You treasured in your heart your ideal of a woman; why could you not have lived so that you would have been her ideal too, when at last you met?" (Grand, *The Heavenly Twins*, 1893) p.346. (New York: Cassell). (16/5.6.1893)

Mary described it as an **extraordinary book,** a difficult remark to interpret but probably indicating, not only amazement at an unfamiliar idea, but also some level of disapproval. (16/5.6.1893)

After the 'fallen woman', the recently emerged 'Girl of the Period,' satirised by Eliza Lynn Linton provides another model, described in this disparaging fashion by Linton.

> "The Girl of the Period is a girl who dyes her hair and paints her face, as the first articles of her personal religion - a creature whose sole idea of life is fun; whose sole aim is unbounded luxury; and whose dress is the sole object of such thought and intellect as she possesses ... and as she lives to please herself, she does not care if she displeases everyone else."

Mary does not record that she read this essay which was published in 1868 in *Saturday Review* but, socially aware as she was, she would have known of such women. Linton's criticisms are echoed by others:

> "For as a rule those men who are most given to flirting with fast women, object the most strongly to marry them." (Fraser, *A Fatal Passion*, 1884) vol 1, p.46. (1879). (13/30.4.1884)

> "Like most men of his calibre, he had a horror of women who were loud. ...This ideal was, after all, a hackneyed one, and one which has existed in the masculine mind since the deluge- a gentle, graceful, feminine abstraction, hedged about with a divine atmosphere of high breeding and heavenly virtue" (Fraser, *A Fatal Passion*, 1884) vol 1, p.89. (1879). (13/30.4.1884)

Another model, less despised but nonetheless often treated with some derision, is that of the 'bluestocking,' not a new label but one dating from the 18th Century. Mary was herself a very well-read woman but she was undemonstrative in her pursuit of book knowledge and read in a family context rather than as a member of a female côterie.

The following comments occur in John Doran's biography of Mrs Elizabeth Montagu, *A Lady of the Last Century*:

> "That card-playing against which intellectual ladies were beginning to set their faces and close their doors." p.265. (9/10.2.1873)

> "Mrs Montagu, a year before she acquired that name, had expressed her distaste for the flashy conversation of her time." p.267. (9/10.2.1873)

> "Mrs. Montagu was not the only lady who gave those literary breakfasts." p.269. (9/10.2.1873)

> "This idea of 'conversation' in place of gambling and other fashionable follies, was the leading idea with the ladies who share the merit of having founded the Bluestocking assemblies." p.273. (9/10.2.1873)

However, ingrained sexist attitudes persisted.

> "After the Byron episode, Miss Blushford began telling her pupil that it was unfeminine as well as unladylike to read much;" (Gray, *In the Heart of the Storm*, 1891) p.69. (New York: United States Book Company). (15/27.5.1891)

A further model is that of 'The New Woman', a broader and

more refined category than Girl of The Period, and including the movement for women's suffrage (thus inclusive of Mary); it had fewer negative connotations and was often less distinct, but represented in various ways the empowerment of women:

> "Even when the spirit of feminine independence after marriage does not assume quite so emancipated a form as this, it very often asserts itself in a manner comparatively new to English society." (Escott, England: Its People, Polity, and Pursuits, 1880) p.309 (Chapman and Hall, 1891). (12/20.6.1880)

> "There are no philanthropic, artistic, or political movements now in which women do not take an interest ... champions of all that is good and just and beautiful Women do not shrink from publicity now as they did a few years ago." (Greville; Adams, The Gentlewoman in Society, 1892) p.32. (15/26.12.1891)

> "But ladies are not contented to work only for others; they aspire to a fuller, a more individual life of their own." (Greville; Adams, The Gentlewoman in Society, 1892) p.33. (15/26.12.1891)

Mary's position was neither categorically feminist nor antifeminist, and it would be a mistake to classify her in this way, but she did seem unconsciously to accept the condescension of men; to feel that women were not necessarily entitled to higher esteem and needed to 'deserve' it; also that they had a separate role within a family.

Below are some quotes from Mary's reading which could be considered by modern standards to have some sexist content, either by denigrating women or suggesting they should occupy a restricted place in society. Many of these, according to the evidence of the diaries, might not have unduly upset her. However, whilst she did not consciously either notice or object to such a constant stream of misogyny meeting her from all directions, not least from women writers, speculation arises as to the subconscious effect of this bombardment of contempt and discrimination on both herself and other women, both in life and literature.

To reiterate, some of the words below are spoken by fictional characters in non-sexist novels where, perhaps, other characters speak with different voices, or where the overall message is mixed; some biographical authors are quoting their subjects; some of the writers are merely describing the current social situation:

> "Don't try to be a man when you are only a woman; and don't set up to preach when you are only called upon to practise." (Sewell, *The Experience of Life*, 1853) p.302. (1858). (2/19.10.1853)

> "'Always meet your husband with a smile,; said the wise

man." (Gordon, *Work, or, Plenty to Do and How to Do It*, 1854) p.42. (3/2.9.1855)

"The mission of the single woman, is, in a great measure, to her own sex. There is a reproach hanging over it which she alone can take away." (Gordon, *Work, or, Plenty to Do and How to Do It*, 1854) p.47. (3/2.9.1855)

"I may be thought to speak harshly of the female character, but whatever persuasion I have of its intended distinction from that of man, I esteem a woman, who only aims to be what God designed her to be, as honourable as any man on earth. She stands not in the same order of excellence, but she is equally honourable. But women have made themselves, and weak men have contributed to make them, what God never designed them to be. Let any thinking man survey the female character as it now stands- often nervous, debilitated, and imaginative, and this super-induced chiefly by education and manners- and he will find it impossible that any great vigor of mind can be preserved, or any high intellectual pursuits cultivated, so far as this character stands in his way." (Cecil; Pratt, *The life and Remains of the Rev. Richard Cecil*, 1854). pp.236-237. (London: Printed for Seeley, 1816). (3/28.9.1856)

"'Doing as others do' is the prevalent principle of the present female character, to whatever absurd, preposterous, masculine, or even wicked lengths it may lead. ... A studious man, whose time is chiefly spent at home, and especially a minister, ought not to have to meet the imaginary wants of his wife. The disorders of an imaginative mind are beyond calculation. ... If she comes not up to the full standard, she will so far impede him, derange him, un-sanctify him." (Cecil; Pratt, *The life and Remains of the Rev. Richard Cecil*, 1854). p.237. (London: Printed for Seeley, 1816). (3/28.9.1856)

"Now, out of tenderness for your feminine ignorance, I must state that, in order to take an observation, it is necessary to get a sight of the sun at a particular moment of the day: this moment is noon." (Dufferin, *Letters from High Latitudes*, 1857) p. 336. (4/14.1.1858)

"Mental doubt rarely touches women. Soldiers and sailors do not doubt. Their religion is remarkable for its simplicity and childlike character." (Robertson, *Sermons*, 2nd Series, 1855 -17 The First Miracle) (Robertson, *Sermons Preached at Brighton, by the late Rev. Frederick W. Robertson*, New York: Harper, 1905) p.386. (1860 onwards)

"Every woman, or at least almost every woman, in England has, at one time or another of her life, charge of the personal health of somebody, whether child, or invalid,- in other words, every woman is a nurse." (Nightingale, *Nightingale's Notes on Nursing*, 1860) p.3. (Preface) (1859). (5/22.2.1860)

"I am not describing all ladies - not those who soberly and piously do home duties first, and find time to help the clergy afterwards; but only the silly daughters of silly mothers, who *know no home duties ... .*" (Pycroft, *Twenty Years in the Church*, 1860) p.10. (1859). (5/16.11.1860)

"*Ellen is pretty well broken in,*" said my father. (Pycroft, *Twenty Years in the Church*, 1860) p.220. (1859). (5/16.11.1860)

"It is well that a man should kneel in spirit before the grace and weakness of a woman, but it is not well that he should kneel either in spirit or body if there be neither grace nor weakness. ... The happy privileges with which women are at present blessed have come to them from the spirit of chivalry. That spirit has taught men to endure in order that women may be at their ease; and has generally taught women to accept the ease bestowed on them with grace and thankfulness. But in America the spirit of chivalry has sunk deeper among men than it has among women ... The conduct of men to women throughout the States is always gracious. ... Women of this class understand their rights but not their duties." (Trollope, *North America*, 1862) pp.190-191. (New York: Harper). (6/9.11.1863)

"That the young women want to get married. God forbid that they should not so want. Indeed God has forbidden in a very express way that there should be any lack of such a desire on the part of women ..." (Trollope, *North America*, 1862) p.255. (New York: Harper). (6/9.11.1863)

"That women should have their rights no man will deny. To

my thinking neither increase of work nor increase of political influence are among them. The best right a woman has is the right to a husband." (Trollope, North America, 1862) p.262. (New York: Harper). (6/9.11.1863)

"Lest she, too, should let the precious season of hay-harvest run by without due use of her summer's sun." (Trollope, The Small House at Allington, 1864) p.130. (Routledge, 1900). (7/18.10.1864)

"Women have less interest in great topics, and less knowledge of them" (Helps, Friends in Council, 1857) vol 1, p.158. (Parker, 1857). (7/24.8.1864)

"It is a narrow view of things to suppose that a just cultivation of women's mental powers will take them out of their sphere: it will only enlarge that sphere." (Friends in Council, 1859) vol 1, p.160. (Parker 1857). (7/24.8.1864)

"For women are often educated in a way to avoid method and intellectual strength of any kind- are probably contented with what the circulating library affords, and read according to the merest rumour and fashion of the present hour." (Helps, Friends in Council, 1859) vol 1, p.264. (Parker, 1857). (7/24.8.1864)

"The masculine is kept distinct from the feminine, for the masculine is the principle of motion, and is higher and more *god-like, whereas the feminine represents only the substance."* (Lewes, *Aristotle*, 1864) p.349. (7/19.11.1864)

"The woman being destined for the part of a nurse and a mother to the world, and the man for the father and governor of the world." Irving, Edward, *Miscellanies from the Collected Writings of Edward Irving* (London: Strahan, 1865) p.129. (7/29.1.1865)

"The unconscious restraint in which most women, even the most violent, are held by the presence of a man, and especially such a man as the master." (Craik, *Christian's Mistake*, 1865) p.184. (New York: Harper). (7/4.4.1865)

"Good substantial wedded affection was not lacking, but romantic love was thought an unnecessary preliminary, and found a vent in extravagant adoration, not always in reputable quarters. Obedience first to the father. Then to the husband, was the first requisite; love might shift for itself." (Yonge, *The Dove in the Eagle's Nest*, 1866) vol 2, p.41. (7/24.7.1866)

"Perhaps a woman never appears to such advantage as when tending the sick, moving gently through the room, or bending tenderly over the couch of the sufferer." (Melville, *Holmby House*, 1866) p.127. (1860). (8/28.3.1869)

"A man who is a nobody can perhaps make himself somebody,- or, at any rate, he can try; but a woman has no means of trying. She is a nobody, and a nobody she must remain."

(Trollope, *He Knew He Was Right*, 1869) p.284. (1870). (8/20.9.1869)

"I don't know what young women in these days have come to," continued Miss Stanbury. "There is no respect, no subjection, no obedience and, too often, - no modesty." (Trollope, *He Knew He Was Right*, 1869). p.321. (1870). (8/20.9.1869)

"We in England are not usually favourably disposed to women who take a pride in a certain antagonism to men in general, and who are anxious to shew the world that they can get on very well without male assistance; ... The hope in regard to all such women, ... is that they will be cured at last by a husband and half-a-dozen children." (Trollope, *He Knew He Was Right*, 1869) p.423. (1870) (8/20.9.1869)

"Freshness, you see, is every thing. The girl's got the dew of the morning on her still" (Aïdé, Hamilton, *Penruddocke*, 1873) p.102. (Boston: Osgood). (9/5.11.1873)

"I hope when I get upon my legs in the House, the image of my wife with a vote won't rise up and choke me!" (Aïdé, Hamilton, *Penruddocke*, 1873) p.102. (Boston: Osgood). (9/5.11.1873)

"The tendency of the masculine intellect is towards inquiry; that of the feminine intellect is towards receptiveness. ... Moreover, what the highest Intelligence of the nation is, the prevalent masculine intelligence of the nation is assuredly on the way to become." (Greg, *Rocks Ahead*, 1874) p.134. (1875). (10/6.3.1875)

"Now, you certainly cannot make young ladies barristers or attorneys; nor employ their brains in getting up cases, civil or criminal; and as for chemistry ... But you may make them something of botanists, zoologists, geologists." (Kingsley, *Health and Education*, 1875) p.140. (1874). (10/23.3.1875)

"I should have thought that it was the glory of woman that she was sent into the world to live for others, rather than for herself. ... something more necessary than the claiming of rights, and that is, the performing of duties ... something more than intellect, and that is purity and virtue. Let her never be persuaded to forget that her calling is not the lower and more earthly one of self-assertion, but the higher and the diviner calling of self-sacrifice ... And if any should answer that this doctrine would keep woman a dependant and a slave, I rejoin- Not so: it would keep her what she should be- the mistress of all around her, because mistress of herself." (Kingsley, *Health and Education*, 1875) p.147. (1874). (10/23.3.1875)

"The woman's part should be to cultivate the affections and the imagination; the man's the intellect of their common soul." (Kingsley; Kingsley, *Charles Kingsley: His Letters and Memories of His Life*, 1877) vol 1, p.65. (11/1.4.1877)

"Those things, combined with the opinion I have formed of the generality of women, who appear to me as children to whom I would rather give a sugar-plum than my time, form a barrier against matrimony which I rejoice in." (Keats; Colvin, *Letters of John Keats to Fanny Brawne*, 1878) p.xxxiv. (New York: Scribner, Armstrong). (11/24.5.1878)

"Better too few words from the woman we love, than too many; while she is silent, Nature is working for her; while she talks, she is working for herself." (Holmes, *The Autocrat of the Breakfast Table*, 1883) p.236. (13/23.9.1883)

"That our girls are in quest of husbands, and know well in what way their lines in life should be laid, is a fact which none can dispute. Let men be taught to recognise the same truth as regards themselves, and we shall cease to hear of the necessity of a new career for women." (Trollope, *The Vicar of Bullhampton*, 1870) p.223. (13/21.3.1884)

"Have nothing left to do but to wish them all good husbands." (Cowper, *Letters of William Cowper*, 1884) p.286. (1907). (13/23.2.1886)

"This is a doctrine unacceptable to men in general; for almost all believe, if even they do not openly maintain, that a woman's love rightfully includes her mental subjection; and that 'she to God through him' is the very norm of wholesome human life." (Lynn, *The Autobiography of Christopher Kirkland*, 1885) vol 3, p.294. (14/13.3.1886)

"A few years of school, and then, how to get a husband-the same then, as it is now, and ever will be." (Ashton, *The Dawn of the XIXth Century in England*, 1886) vol 2, p.60. (14/9.5.1886)

"Girls stop at home and help in the house. They can make and mend their own clothes, don't stop out o' nights, or want setting up in business." (Westall, *A Fair Crusader*, 1888) p.166. (Spencer Blackett & Hallam, 1889). (14/20.1.1888)

"Since when had young women put on all these airs? In his young days they knew their place." (Ward, *Robert Elsmere*, 1888) p.160. (15/3.12.1888)

"He doesn't like women to talk about books. He says they only pretend- even the clever ones. Except, of course, Madame de Stael. He can only say she was ugly, and I don't deny it." (Ward, *Robert Elsmere*, 1888) p.213. (15/3.12.1888)

"There is something so absurd, so unpleasant, in a young woman's meddling with things which don't belong to her, in seeing a little mind struggle with ideas. Better a thousand times settle down to look after her household, and cook her husband's dinner, and be a good child." (Deland, *John Ward, Preacher*, 1889) p.191. (Boston: Houghton Mifflin, 1888). (15/31.5.1889)

"It's very unfeminine to think, and Gifford is so clever, he doesn't stop to remember she's but a woman." (Deland, *John

Ward, Preacher, 1889) p.193. (Boston: Houghton Mifflin, 1888). (15/31.5.1889)

"For Mr Grier held with St Paul that the husband was head of the wife, even to the extent of regulating her conscience;" (Deland, John Ward, Preacher, 1889) p.301. (Boston: Houghton Mifflin, 1888). (15/31.5.1889)

"'Well, you must believe it, then,' the rector said, striking his fist on the arm of his chair; 'it is the wife's place to yield; and while I acknowledge it is all folly, you must give in.'" (Deland, John Ward, Preacher, 1889) p.391. (Boston: Houghton, Mifflin, 1888). (15/31.5.1889)

"The ordinary disposition of women is to respect what is authorized much more than what is original" (Hamerton, Human Intercourse, 1889). p.49. (1884). (15/6.9.1889)

"Women indulge in confusions even more frequently than men, and are less disposed to separate things when they have once been jumbled together." (Hamerton, Human Intercourse, 1889). p.266. (1884). (15/6.9.1889)

"Women who are not impelled by some masculine influence are not superior either in knowledge or in discipline of mind, at the age of fifty to what they were at twenty-five." (Hamerton, Human Intercourse, 1889) p.361. (1884). (15/6.9.1889)

"I am of the old-fashioned patriarchal way of thinking; I

regard the wife as the appanage of the husband." (McCarthy, Linley Rochford, 1890) p.75. (15/1.9.1891)

"A very little wit is valued in a woman, as we are pleased with a few words spoken plain by a parrot." (Hay, Swift: The Mystery of His Life and Love, 1891) p.241. (15/10.1.1892)

The following quotations come not only from a point of view at odds with the conservative position expressed above, but with a clear voice of protest, and Mary could have been uncomfortable with some of them, as she seemed to be with *The Heavenly Twins*, because they hinted of rebellion.

"You treat me like an equal; you will deign to argue with me. But men in general- oh, they hide their contempt for us, if not their own ignorance, under that mask of chivalrous deference!" (Kingsley, Yeast, 1851) p.30. (New York: Harper). (2/10.3.1852)

"They (journalists) write as if woman's whole existence was comprised between fifteen and the fading of her bloom or beauty. If they talk of her devotion, it must be associated, not with ideas of duty, reverence, and piety, but with a hint how much it lights up her features. She is recommended good humour, because it will preserve her complexion; and a modest dress and demeanour, because!!! they are more attractive than any other, even in the eyes of the greatest libertines." (Trench, *The Remains of the Late Mrs. Richard Trench*, 1862) pp.505-506. (6/25.9.1862)

"*Campe's book, 'A Father's Advice to his Daughters,' made a great impression on me at that time. Marriage was there represented as the only proper destiny for a girl, and something within me secretly protested against this view.*" (Poel; Winkworth, *Life of Amelia Wilhelmina Sieveking*, 1863) pp.159-160. (6/2.1.1864)

"*Holding women in subjection, by representing to them meekness, submissiveness, and resignation of all individual will into the hands of a man, as an essential part of sexual attractiveness.*" (Mill, *The Subjection of Women*, 1870) p.28. (8/22.5.1870) (book finished on this date)

"*In the present day, power holds a smoother language, and whomsoever it oppresses, always pretends to do so for their own good.*" (Mill, *The Subjection of Women*, 1870) p.92. (8/22.5.1870) (book finished on this date)

"*We must stay where we grow, or where the gardeners like to transplant us. We are brought up like the flowers, to look as pretty as we can, and be dull without complaining. That is my notion about the plants: they are often bored, and that is the reason why some of them have got poisonous,*" (Eliot, *Daniel Deronda*, 1876) vol 1, p.242. (10/10.4.1876)

"*You may try but you can never imagine what it is to have a man's force of genius in you, and yet to suffer the slavery of being a girl.*" (Eliot; Cross, *George Eliot's Life as Related* in her *Letters and Journals*, between 1878 and 1885) vol 1, p.34. (1885). (11.6.1879)

"*If we ascribe the book to a woman at all, we have no alternative but to ascribe it to one who has for some sufficient reason long forfeited the society of her own sex.*" The world knows the truth now. It knows that these bitter and shameful words were applied to one of the truest and purest of women; to a woman who from birth had led a life of self-sacrifice and patient endurance; etc etc." (Reid, *Charlotte Brontë*, 1877) p.12. (12/14.11.1879)

"*She had never quite escaped from the notion that in putting pen to paper she was in some vague way offending against the proprieties of society.*" (Reid, *Charlotte Brontë*, 1877) p.185. (12/14.11.1879)

"*Why a woman should not be allowed to choose her husband as freely as a husband chooses his wife.*" (Oliphant, *Altiora Peto*, 1883, New York: Harper) p.11. (13/27.11.1883)

"*And what did any good woman want more than a baby, and buttons to sew on to her husband's shirts? Well-regulated women never require equal companionship, interchange of ideas, sympathy, consideration, and love, if the husband withhold these boons. Thus, if at times the proud strong nature of the woman, the rich reserve of generous emotions, rose up in conscious antagonism to the stagnation of her existence, and fought and struggled passionately in her pure breast for the* mastery, who was any the wiser? She smote her fair bosom in self-accusing penitence, ate out her heart in solitude, and went on from day to day, from year to year, along the straight unquestioned path of duty." (Bothmer, *Aut Caesar Aut Nihil*, 1883) vol 1, pp.25-26. (13/ 29.11.1883)

"Mellin had always felt that to utilise the enthusiasm and power of women would be to turn to account a glut of undeveloped capital lying dormant for want of a motive power sufficiently strong to set it going." (Bothmer, *Aut Caesar Aut Nihil*, 1883) vol 1, p.242. (13/29.11.1883)

"'Doesn't a woman expect to be guided by her husband?' "Mr Dale asked. 'When he has sense enough,' responded his wife significantly." (Deland, *John Ward, Preacher*, 1889) p.473. (Boston: Houghton, Mifflin, 1888). (15/31.5.1889)

"All the fiends in hell could not cause more suffering than is sometimes inflicted by a man, for his own amusement, upon the unhappy woman whom he has promised to love and to cherish. More commonly, however, selfishness shows itself by simple indifference." (Momerie, *Preaching and Hearing*, 1888) p.144. (1890). (15/20.10.1889)

"Hope good women who live in this dutiful routine get to like it, and find a happiness in the thought of so much humble handmaiden's work performed so steadily; but to the profane and the busy it seems hard thus to wear away a life."

(Oliphant, *The Curate in Charge*, 1885) p.16 (1883). (15/21.2.1890)

"I should like to be a man if only to have a chance of being a member of Parliament. Do you know that one of the longings of my life is to hear a debate in the House of Commons; to be in the Ladies' gallery and hear a debate?" (McCarthy; Praed, *The Ladies' Gallery*, 1890) p.59. (New York: Appleton, 1889). (15/14.2.1891)

"But Ada was only a woman, she had not had the advantage of hearing men of the world instruct each other upon the different code of ethics proper to each sex, as Philip had; and having early discovered that conventional morality is, for the most part, a hybrid between real morality and the expediency invented by ages of male selfishness, resolved to accept none not based upon justice and truth." (Gray, *In the Heart of the Storm*, 1891) p.69. (New York: United States Book Company). (15/27.5.1891)

"But for Margaret she would have fallen at once into the domestic drudge which was all Drumcarro understood or wanted in a wife." (Oliphant, *Kirsteen*, 1891). vol 1, p.81. (London: Macmillan, 1890). (15/9.7.1891)

"Rochford married her out of a whim, thinking he had got a pretty little toy to play with, and then put away on the shelf until he wanted it again." (McCarthy, *Linley Rochford*, 1890). p.119. (15/1.9.1891)

> "He thought women inferior to men, that they should be in subjection to them, should give way to them, should be content with their own part in the world- and their part was first to be pretty and submissive and charming, and then as they grew older to be drudges, or if not exactly that, to look after home, to mother children, and leave the rest of life to the stronger sex." (Clifford, Love-letters of a Worldly Woman, 1892) p.105. (15/27.4.1892)

> "Now that I am older and see clearly, I know well enough how to measure the strength of the masterful man- it does not take long. I know his inward grudgingness towards women, his shallowness, his unconscious fear of being found out." (Clifford, Letters of a Worldly Woman, 1892) pp. 105-106. (15/27.4.1892)

> "The words 'home' and 'prison' are pretty well synonymous in the case of some women." (Malet, Counsel of Perfection, 1888) p.169. (15/7.7.1892)

> "She was called upon to sacrifice so much- her individual hopes and cravings; called upon to mutilate her personality so as to fit it into a mould altogether too narrow and small for it." (Malet, Counsel of Perfection, 1888) pp.230-231. (15/7.7.1892)

We have seen that extremely misogynistic statements drew comment from Mary, but even then she did not seem outraged.

It is worth repeating that, although the atmosphere of gender discrimination was pervasive, Mary suffered little in her life that was directly oppressive and, after a typically 'sulky' adolescence, religious and social forces encouraged her compliance. Misfortunes such as her younger sister's tragic death, and her struggle in widowhood to retain the family estates were, in fact, responsible for much of the unhappiness she suffered, as was her own self-critical nature.

It is fascinating that a highly intelligent woman, reading so much controversial material concerning gender, seems to have been so little influenced or even disturbed by it. As with her reading of religious controversies, it may illustrate how she lived life emotionally and intuitively, grasping the arguments but proceeding quietly along her own pathway with the conviction that this was the way God beckoned.

7

Suffocation

It is strange how little we imagine in our youth, when the path of life is woven of the sunbeam and the rainbow, how deeply and bitterly we may yet weep in after life. But till those tears or their equivalent come on us, we are not yet men, but children.
(Brooke, Sermons Preached in St. James Chapel) p.24. (1871)
(12/16.11.1880)

A sort of weight of depression had been gradually creeping on me & increasing at the termination of each morning's duties... I could not have slept long before I woke in a state of suffocation- struggling hard for breath, I was glad when it was over and no one had seen me.
Mary's Diaries (24.7.1843)

Mary's terrified words were written nine days after hearing that Lord Strathavon was planning to present her with a tartan, presumably to initiate her entry into his Scottish family prior to making her his wife. Perhaps, although no negative feelings towards him are apparent from the diaries, this gripped her with a feeling of unavoidable destiny. The notion of hidden sorrows to come, as expressed above by the preacher, Stopford Brooke, is commonplace in Mary's books.

Note also:

> "People wish to know the future at the beginning; if the wish were granted, three-fourths of us would go mad." (Sewell, *The Experience of Life*, 1853) p.274. (1858). (2/19.10.1853)

> "Well is it for us that we cannot foresee the destinies of our children; merciful the blindness that shuts out from us the long perspective of the future- the coming struggles we should none of us have courage to confront." (Melville, *Holmby House*, 1866) p.197. (1860). (8/28.3.1869)

> "Happy it is for us that we can never see the future!" (Grant, *Lady Wedderburn's Wish*, 1870) p.402. (Routledge 1871). (9/15.11.1870)

How often, these are all saying, it is a blessing for us not to be aware of the misfortunes ahead. Mary, in her youth, had visions of sadness ahead:

> Every lovely herb & flower & even the rich foliage of the trees I thus admire, must soon suffer beneath the chilling blast of winter & days roll on & the autumnal breeze sweeps with a low moan over the graves of departed sweets. ... It is unnecessary to apply these reflections to that Christian hope which will triumphant shine above every trial of life. (23.10.1841)

However, perhaps she did not anticipate the depths of sorrow into which she would sink.

The theme of suffocation ran through her life experiences, appearing in various guises. To return to some features of her life, although Mary and Charlotte's privileged upbringing included some awareness of other environments and other scenarios, it was in the process of growing to full adulthood that they were forced to deal with them. Progressing beyond childhood years, Charlotte began to renounce her childhood idyll in the garden at Uffington. On her marriage to John Guest, owner of a massive iron foundry in Dowlais, South Wales, she entered a very different landscape and culture. She adapted herself to the new surroundings, turning landscape into lived space. Though, like Mary, she had often felt alienated in city environments, she now made regular visits to London, continuing to maintain her place in society.

Not so Mary. Continuing to dislike all urban and industrial environments, she found it unbearable even to visit her sister in industrial Wales, as she did around the time of her twenty-first birthday. She voiced her anxieties about the devastated landscape:

> *Nearer to Dowlais, I need not observe that all signs of verdure ceased and that the steam rose fogging & rolling, the thousand wheels rushed round & the furnaces blazed in their wonted glory! I endeavoured the same evening to represent all this in my sketchbook with a brush & some lamp black the only colour necessary excepting red and yellow for the flames.* (22.4.1843)

Mary admitted to a state of denial about this visual affront. A few days later, she reported many *descents from the carriage to pick orchises, cowslips, primroses, and other wayside flowers, by which time I had well nigh recovered the powers of admiring.* (27.4.1843). Later she amplified her half-brother's more emotionally muted and intellectually framed expressions as they journeyed together:

> *Berties' questions & observations were amusing & instructive nothing escaped his notice, - & he was affected with a fit of despondency at the occurrence of every little waste piece of land – as well as the vallies left by the cinders tip. I believe he was gradually becoming absorbed in a computation- how many years it would take him with a spud to reduce the face of the country into a level, for the purpose of substituting pleasant fields in the place of barren wastes.* (15.8.1843)

Whilst all this may appear as simple revulsion to the industrial landscape, it was not so simple. Mary was capable of ambivalence and of aesthetic responses to apparently ugly scenes and her descriptions, whilst fraught with horror, nonetheless give a value to the brilliant contrasts, as when she reported, *The displays of gorgeous light orange red & blue of one of the cindertips was dazzlingly beautiful ... .* (30.8.1843). But her feelings, prompted by the human implications, became apparent following a trip down one of the mines at Dowlais. She related, *We all saw the miners conveyed from the pits by the same easy method of transition. All very novel very astonishing, & very awful.* She described *suffocating smoke and deafening noises.*(11.8.1843). Twenty years later, she would speak of a mining accident in the news: *Mr. Cooke preached upon the awful calamity in the Hartley Colliery. 215 men buried alive ... they must have lingered alive many days hoping to be rescued.* (5/26.1.1862). Perhaps the slag heaps, encountered in Wales, foretold the suffocating dross that would be poured at intervals on Mary's life as it progressed, and that would be attributed more often than not to God's chastening, though loving, Hand.

Sadly, the theme of suffocation was a persistent one in her life: the death of her younger sister by drowning at age 13; her husband's death, coughing and choking with lung disease; the death of Lewie, one of her sons, by drowning in a sinking naval vessel, and of Douglas whose chest had been crushed in a number of riding accidents. Images of claustrophobia and suffocation also occurred frequently in relation to social environments, which stifled Mary. She mentioned a trip to Almack's, the social meeting rooms for the elite in London, declaring that she *found it hot crowded and miserable.* (21.6.1843). Describing a ball at Burghley, she wrote, *It was dreadfully crowded.* **Prince Albert came up & asked to be introduced to me & Strath obliged.** (1/14.11.1844)

In almost any life there is a catalogue of sorrows and at least a few disasters, so maybe Mary was not exceptional in this regard. Possibly some of the problems could be laid at her own door. Maybe her charming unworldliness and her reliance on heavenly reward had a downside for her more worldly family. A firmer hand in the household and, especially with her more wayward children, and a better grasp of business matters could have improved the family's situation after Strath's death. Her over-conservative views and humble submission to the evangelistic view of woman might have weakened her ability to handle the family's problems. Possibly she was a little envious of Charlotte's freedom. Maybe she was governed by some simple failings and excesses, in spite of all she read and all her intellectual abilities. Thus the world suffocated her, her children suffocated her with blame, and, sometimes, she also suffocated herself.

There were 'suffocating' features of the times in which Mary lived, such as the encroachment of cities and the development of industry and technology. The latter could be a mixed blessing, although railways, to which there was great initial opposition, came ultimately to be felt as a blessing by most people, including Mary. In cultural terms there was the increasing pace of life, the expansion of print culture (a huge blessing in enabling the democratisation of learning but also productive of much detritus), changes in the social order - Chartism, feminism, decline of the landed aristocracy, and, perhaps most of all, the turbid tide of scepticism, breeding agnosticism and despair.

To play devil's advocate and pursue 'cup half full,' one could ask incredulously, what sadness should be felt for Mary? She had a privileged life with possessions and power that few, lower in the social hierarchy could even dream of. Whilst some of her children perished early, most of them reached adulthood and some flourished and led full lives. She had the leisure to fulfil her desires, to garden, write a little, travel when she wanted, and to read massively. She had good and knowledgeable friends and family and a husband who loved her and blest her with beautiful estates which she kept for at least her lifetime. What about the many lives whose potential is blighted and those with literally nothing- those in great pain, those with no faith? It might be suggested that privileges bring burdens and responsibilities and maybe Mary just got buffeted by the wind. All this is inarguable; sorrow is a relative thing. However, the sadness presented here is a special kind of sadness experienced by Mary and all too often by us; it is the sadness of loss, the gradual withdrawal of the dearest things in life, the obliteration of dreams.

For Mary, also, there were stresses in the social scene, - in the ballroom, the London season, the formal visiting programmes, the coming out of daughters. These were certainly not exclusively nineteenth century features and many women thrived on such excitement, but Mary, alongside other women of a less frivolous nature, found such obligations very tiresome.

To an extent, Mary's 'suffocation' was a result of her own lack of confidence and adaptability, but she did fight back. Her vigorous quest for freedom led her out into her large gardens and the boundless wilds around her estates, and abroad, in pursuit of fresh air and natural beauty, digging, weeding, scrambling up inclines and voraciously collecting her real treasures, overreaching her class and her gender in her physical efforts. It also led her to libraries, newspapers and intellectual associates in search of a great range of reading material, including some of the most controversial and intellectually challenging. As, in body, she wandered far and free in her gardening and botanising, so in mind she did the same with her reading. Whilst maintaining social conventionalities and her heartfelt beliefs, she roamed endlessly in imagination.

The landscape of the country estate, with its conservative values of aestheticism, rural life, nation, family and religion, provided Mary with stability, and her happy self was linked to the beautiful gardens and surroundings of her country homes. She adapted in a brave but limited way to the stresses of her life and, especially, to the threat of bankruptcy after husband's death. She struggled with the demands of an evolving world, but a number of bereavements devastated her and she lost much of the family's land in England and Scotland. Whilst not a 'committed' aristocrat, she was, nonetheless, part of a grand narrative that was in decline.

Dwellers in the twenty-first century suffer in excess from many of the factors Mary found difficult to bear- the pace of life, the blight of natural environments, the tyrannies of materialism and social pressures. Mary was caught in the transition. Her world was turned upside down many times over; no wonder that her religious instincts prevailed and she turned over and over again to her Christian obedience. Her spiritual journey took her in a straight and undeviating line from birth to death, though her intellectual journey took her through belief and scepticism, through heaven and hell.

My acquaintance with Mary through her diaries is now a lengthy one and, although I do not follow all her religious practices, she has greatly assisted me on my own journey of Christian faith, impressed as I have been by the staunchness of hers. I did not suffer the shock of her contemporaries at the scholarly and scientific discoveries which so often undermined religious faith, but I have lived in an age long secular which has tended to sap belief. Less disgusted than she at all that is urban and industrial, I have followed her into garden and countryside. I am only glad that, between and amidst the throes of suffocation, through her gardens and wildflowers and her books and, supremely through her Christian aspirations, Mary was able to breathe and live.

Uffington House, Stamford
From Gertrude Jekyll and Christopher Hussey 'Garden Ornament', 2nd edn., [S.I.] (Country Life 1927, 1st 1918)

Uffington Lodges
Lincolnshire Archives, Misc Don 298/8

Ordnance Survey Map of Uffington Estate
1883-1888 (original 25"/mile)

Gates to Uffington Estate: Churchside,
1993
Lincolnshire Archives, Misc Don 680/3

Orton Hall, Northamptonshire
Huntingdonshire Archives and Local Studies, Huntly family album (1860-1870) Huntly/1343/1

The Avenue of Sequoia Gigantea at Orton Hall
From Charles Gordon, 'Auld Acquaintance', London: Hutchinson [1929]

Ordnance Survey Map of Orton Hall and Estate
1882-1887 (original 25"/mile)

ACKNOWLEDGEMENTS

Thanks are due to various sources for this book, especially the Huntingdonshire and Northamptonshire Archives.

www.ingramcontent.com/pod-product-compliance
Lightning Source LLC
Chambersburg PA
CBHW070642120526
44590CB00013BA/823